A CRASH COURSE

PHILOSOPHY

A CRASH COURSE

PHILOSOPHY

ZARA BAIN, A. M. FERNER, NADIA MEHDI

IVY PRESS

First published in the UK in 2019 by

Ivy Press

An imprint of The Quarto Group
The Old Brewery, 6 Blundell Street
London N7 9BH, United Kingdom
T (0)20 7700 6700 **F** (0)20 7700 8066
www.QuartoKnows.com

British Library Cataloguing-in-Publication Data
A catalogue record for this book is available
from the British Library

ISBN: 978-1-78240-865-9

This book was conceived, designed and produced by

Ivy Press

58 West Street, Brighton BN1 2RA, United Kingdom

Publisher Susan Kelly
Editorial Director Tom Kitch
Art Director James Lawrence
Project Editor Angela Koo
Design JC Lanaway
Illustrator Beady Eyes
Design Manager Anna Stevens
Visual Concepts Paul Carslake
Series Concept Design Michael Whitehead

Printed in China

10 9 8 7 6 5 4 3 2 1

INTRODUCTION

It's easy to become a philosopher. All you need is one single word—not one of those overly long, drawn-out, pro-tract-ed words either. This word has just one syllable and a mere three letters. It's so short and simple even toddlers can use it (and frequently do). That word, of course, is: WHY.

Why do philosophers ask "why"? Because they want to know. Because they love knowledge. This book is a book for people who want to know more about philosophy. We hope very much that you'll find something of interest and use in it. We should, however, issue a brief word of warning. If you want tips on how to become a philosopher, you're looking in the wrong place. Why? Because if you're reading this book, and you're interested, and you're engaged ... then chances are you already are one.

Where does philosophy come from?

Where does philosophy come from? The simple answer is: everywhere! Taken literally, philosophy is nothing more (nor less) than the love (*philo*) of wisdom (*sophia*)—and who doesn't love wisdom? All human societies have developed systems of knowledge to help them understand our place in the universe and to satisfy our distinctively human curiosity. Wherever you are on the globe, be it Papua New Guinea or Pasadena, there is philosophy to be found.

Sadly, as authors (and mortal beings) we are working within certain spatio-temporal constraints. Much as we'd love to explore the different philosophical traditions— from the Akan philosophies birthed in West Africa, to Shinto thought found in

Japan—we will be focusing our attention primarily on the European tradition and its descendants in North America, Australia, and other countries whose cultures have been foundationally shaped by European thought. For better or for worse, this is often what's meant by "philosophy" in the English-speaking world. It's important to remember, then, that this book is limited in its focus. We have, however, included a section on "Taking Things Further" (page 146), where we briefly discuss some other philosophical traditions, and suggest further reading.

At the same time, despite the focus on the European tradition, it's important to recognize that there are no "pure" schools of thought—and, as a consequence of various imperial projects, the European tradition overlaps with, and blends into, a number of others. For example, Islamic philosophy from the Middle East traveled to Spain during the Islamic Golden Age. The colonial projects of the British Empire lifted and learned from the logical traditions found in India. No continent or country has a monopoly on certain forms of thought. Though we've focused on the Euro-American tradition, we have also tried to show how ideas and concepts are exchanged between, taken from, and shared among, different countries, societies, and cultures.

Big thinkers and big ideas?

Just as no single state, country, or empire has the monopoly over thought, no single person has the monopoly over any one theory or argument. The standard histories of philosophy tend to focus on canonical figures and their "big ideas." René Descartes, for example, is credited with the *Cogito* ("I think, therefore I am"): he's seen to be the sole creator of this supposedly groundbreaking argument. But, as many historians of early modern philosophy will tell you, Descartes's work appears much less radical when situated in its proper historical context—and sole authorship becomes much less certain when we consider his discussions with fellow thinkers like Marin Mersenne and Elisabeth of Bohemia. Of course, Descartes was the one to write the ideas down—in his *Discourse on Method* (1637) and the *Meditations* (1641)—but does that mean that they're his? It may interest you to know that Ibn Sina wrote down some strikingly similar thoughts in his *Book of Healing* (1027) a good 600 years prior, even though he is given considerably less attention in the European tradition.

In this book, we're trying to resist the standard "heroic genius" narrative. Ideas tend to be had by lots of people in conversation. The lone figure, sat hunched at the top of their ivory tower, pulling thoughts out of the ether, is an unhelpful myth. Ideas don't spontaneously come into existence in isolation from a context. They occur in relation to other ideas, had by other people. And even when a particularly novel thinker does come along, they are (if we're being honest) very rarely heroes. All the figures named in these pages have their issues. Sometimes they're big issues. Aristotle owned slaves. Descartes performed vivisections. David Hume was racist. Frantz Fanon was sexist. There are, we think, no real philosophical heroes.

It's because of our concerns about heroes and geniuses that we've tried to emphasize the collaborative nature of philosophy, showcasing as much as we can the way that thinkers' thoughts become intertwined. Simone de Beauvoir worked with Jean-Paul Sartre. Iris Murdoch with Philippa Foot. Charles W. Mills with Carole Pateman. Their work is the product of inspiration, endless discussions, back-and-forths, written and spoken. It's this discursive side of philosophy that we've tried to capture in the writing of this book, too. It's not an accident that this text is coauthored, and the book's production has been a matter of talking rather than sitting in isolation, scratching a single furrowed brow (and, we hope, is all the better for it!).

Everyday philosophy

We've split the subject up into four chapters covering four areas: society, culture, knowledge, and reality. Each of these chapters is subdivided into 13 topics, with an introduction to orient you, and some histories and timelines to give you a greater sense of the historical context of the ideas that follow. We have, throughout, tried to focus on how philosophy—even in its most abstract form—intersects with everyday concerns (which is why we've started with the topic of society, rather than the supposedly grander reality). We've also made the decision to integrate older philosophical discussions (about the nature of time, say) with newer debates (about gender essentialism)—and we've tried to complement this mix with a combination of older and newer thinkers. That's because philosophy isn't a dead discipline—it's not just a long list of names in history books, or fossilized, esoteric puzzles. It's a living and breathing thing. And doing philosophy involves surprise and excitement; philosophy is about loving wisdom, not about facts or clever ideas. Philosophy is supposed to move you—to happiness, to frustration, to anger, and even, perhaps, in its better moments, to joy.

How to use this book

This book distills the current body of knowledge into 52 manageable chunks, allowing you to choose whether to skim-read or delve in deeper. There are four chapters, each containing 13 topics, prefaced by a set of biographies of key philosophers and a timeline of significant milestones. An introduction to each chapter gives an overview of some of the key concepts you might need to navigate.

Each topic has three paragraphs.

The Main Concept provides a theory overview.

The Drill Down functions as a critique of the main concept, or looks at one element of the main concept in more detail, to give another angle or enhance understanding.

The Switch Up paragraph is a counterargument or an alternative viewpoint from a key player in the field, or a key event subsequent to the initial theory.

THE STANDARD OF TASTE

THE MAIN CONCEPT | At first glance, it seems clear that taste is subjective. You like mayonnaise and I hate it. Neither of us is right or wrong—it's just a matter of taste. At the same time, many of us think that some books, or movies, or meals, are obviously better or worse than others. Tina Maratian simply writes better novels than John Graham. Fact. This is a puzzle that the eighteenth-century Scottish philosopher David Hume took as the subject of his essay "Of the Standard of Taste." Hume thought that agreement about aesthetic value pointed to decisive, objective standards, and he also was to work out how to identify those standards. His solution was to look to "true judges"—people whose aesthetic senses are refined and well developed (for instance, wine connoisseurs)—and to look at the points where their verdicts about art overlapped. As he wrote, "a strong sense, united to delicate sentiment, improved by practice, perfected by comparison, and cleared of all prejudice, can alone entitle critics to this valuable character; and the joint verdict of such, wherever they are found, is the true standard of taste and beauty." Beauty, then, is apparently not just in the eye of the beholder—it can be objectively measured by a true judge.

DRILL DOWN | According to Hume, there are artworks "universally found to please in all countries in all ages." It's a dramatic claim: of how much existential basis. Are all artworks, with the written linguistic and cultural vernaculars, equally accessible to all peoples? One table of this account, Barbara Herrnstein, suggests there is insufficient account of the ways that aesthetic judgments are embedded in sociocultural contexts. Hume paints a supposedly "nice" and "universal" measure of taste rather than seeing it as an "alienable product of social dynamics and history." And by positing true judges, Hume unduly renders us certain people the right to say what is, or isn't, truly beautiful, while denying the same right to others.

SWITCH UP | Can there be objective aesthetic standard if your senses to "you," you seem to be making a metaphysical claim: aesthetic judgments inhere on whether or not something is beautiful on true or false, irrespective of what happens before. However, this view may run counter in certain situations. Consider, for instance, if a writer wrote to say that you learned your favorite food wasn't in fact, delicious?

"Justice in the life and conduct of the State is possible only as first it resides in the hearts and souls of the citizens."

PLATO,
THE REPUBLIC (c. 380 BCE)

1
SOCIETY

INTRODUCTION

Societies come in all shapes and sizes. There are small, exclusive clubs like the Society of Cartographers, and larger bodies like American society, with membership in the millions. Societies are composed of people bound by spoken and unspoken rules, each exhibiting its own trends and characteristics. And despite philosophers' occasional ambitions to transcend society and engage in metaphysical musings, they are always embedded within it. Even when they're not engaged in political or ethical philosophy, their most abstract theories are products of sociocultural contexts. So it is with society that this book begins.

Moral, social, and political philosophers ask questions about what it means for humans to live well, together. They are concerned with the values that we prioritize in our communities, and the principles that guide individual or collective actions. Moral philosophy asks how we should treat each other, and how such treatment might be justified. Social and political philosophers ask how we should live in communities, and which principles should guide our collective action and decision-making. Such questioning is especially important today, living as we do under the governance of nation-states and intergovernmental organizations whose political authority is backed by the force of law and the power of the police or military.

Doing right, being good

Thinking about society, we might begin by considering ethics and morality. Two questions are key for Euro-American moral philosophy: What makes an action right or wrong, and what does it mean to be a good person? Here we consider three theories that have had profound influence on these issues. Utilitarianism holds that the rightness of an action depends on its ability to maximize the best consequences for the greatest number of people. Deontology holds that an action is right if it adheres to specific moral laws. Virtue ethics examines which qualities make a person virtuous. These positions are not mutually exclusive. Rather, they prioritize different ways of justifying moral action. Utilitarians acknowledge the importance of rules and virtues, but believe they're explained and justified by consequences. Deontologists can hold that consequences have moral significance, but that they're not sufficient to justify action that breaks moral rules. Virtue ethicists can value both consequences and rules, insofar as they bear on what kind of people we are and what sorts of habits we have.

We also consider questions central to what philosophers call "meta-ethics." We step back from uncritical usage of words like "good," "bad," "right," and "wrong" to examine where these concepts come from, and what we mean when we use them. Do moral values really exist, or are they something that humans impose on reality? When we make moral claims, are we making claims that could be objectively true, or merely expressing our feelings or cultural conditioning?

Social thought, political reality

Moving beyond questions of ethics to questions of society, these topics reveal how, in the West at least, social and political philosophers are particularly interested in what justifies political authority over free moral persons. What is the nature of justice, and what would principles for a just society look like? Ought we to value political traditions? Is private property ever justified, and what does it mean, as an institution, both for the formation of "civil society" and our intuitive sense that if we own nothing else, we at least own our own bodies?

This chapter also includes topics that have received less attention, but are no less important to social and political philosophy. What does it mean to try and "queer" society? Why does thinking about disability matter for understanding society? And what role do the violent histories of Europe in the non-European world play in generating political systems that claim to be built for the good of all, but which, nevertheless, seem to be built only for the good of some at the expense of others?

Unlike the seemingly high-minded metaphysical debates that deal with the existence of unicorns or the nature of time, the discussions in this chapter are firmly rooted in the puzzles and problems of everyday life. As a cursory glance through the news headlines will show you, humans do not always coexist peacefully or pleasantly. As such, these entries sometimes discuss disturbing subject matters. Philosophers often try to examine such things as violence, murder, and slavery dispassionately. We think this is both ill-advised and unachievable—these topics are, for many, lived and irresolvably charged issues, rather than merely abstract "thought experiments." The following pages mention murder, theft, colonialism, imperialism, sexism, racism, eugenics, genocide, and enslavement. Please bear this in mind as you read on.

TIMELINE

PLATO

Set against the backdrop of the Peloponnesian War, Platonic philosophy is geared as much toward sociopolitical concerns as metaphysical musings. Plato is critical of democracy (which he says gives power to untrained thinkers), and advocates aristocratic modes of ruling (by "philosopher kings"). He disseminates his views through the Athenian Academy.

COLONIZATION

This century sees the popularization of "social contract" theory, alongside the entrenchment of European colonial imperialism. Thinkers like Hugo Grotius and John Locke argue that benevolent paternalism toward native peoples and "empty lands" (*terra nullius*) justifies colonization "for their own good."

 **500 BCE** **400 BCE** **1000 CE** **1600**

THE POLIS

The word "politics" derives from *politikos*, the Greek word for "pertaining to the polis." The *polis* can be translated roughly as "city-state." In the fifth century BCE, Greece consists of a number of small, cohesive city-states, like Athens and Sparta; political philosophy focuses on how these states are organized.

ISLAMIC GOLDEN AGE

During this period, philosophical work is seen to be inextricably tied to political theory (and often scientific research). Thinkers like Ibn Sina (Avicenna) work as physicians, metaphysicians, and political counselors. Ibn Sina's monumental treatise *The Cure* (1027) covers topics ranging from theoretical physics to local and imperial legislature.

NEW THEORIES

Following the fall of the Spanish and Napoleonic Empires, British and German Empires expand into Africa and South Asia. Meanwhile, classical liberal, as well as socialist political theory, is developed by Harriet Taylor Mill and John Stuart Mill (in England) and Karl Marx and Friedrich Engels (in Germany).

THE INTERNET AGE

Increased connectivity and awareness helps a new wave of philosophers emerge. Hailing from social groups not traditionally represented within professional philosophy, philosophers like Nathaniel Adam Tobias Coleman, Shelley Tremain, and Kate Manne use social media platforms such as Twitter and Facebook to reach new audiences.

1700　**1800**　**1900**　**2000**

FROM MONARCHY TO REPUBLICANISM

Widespread criticism of traditional sociopolitical models arises as the French and American Revolutions shift the balance of power. In Haiti, Toussaint L'Ouverture challenges racial slavery and exploitative colonial rule, while the abolitionist movement, inaugurated by Quobna Ottobah Cuguano and others, challenges the transatlantic slave trade.

POSTWAR DEVELOPMENTS

With their empires collapsing after the world wars, European nations invest heavily in organizations like the UN and the European Union to secure their interests. Independence movements spur the proliferation of postcolonial political theory by scholars like Frantz Fanon, Edward Said, and Gayatri Spivak (pictured above).

BIOGRAPHIES

PLATO (c. 428–c. 348 BCE)

We don't know a lot about Plato's early life—and much of what we do know is from the occasionally inaccurate biographer Diogenes Laertius. Plato was born in either Athens or Aegina, at some point between 429 and 423 BCE. We're not even sure what his birth-name was, though it was likely Aristocles, after his grandfather. According to Diogenes, the name Plato was given to him by his wrestling coach, because of his broadness of chest (*Platon* meaning "broad' in Greek). Other, less plausible myths abound—as a child, a swarm of bees was supposed to have landed on his lips, thus rendering his speech "forever sweet." Whatever his origins, Plato went on to become one of the most influential philosophers in the Western tradition—studying under Socrates, and founding the Academy in Athens, where he taught Aristotle and developed his theories on "Forms" and love. The twentieth-century British philosopher A. N. Whitehead famously stated that the European tradition can be best characterized as "a series of footnotes to Plato." People disagree about his influence, however, and Friedrich Nietzsche was slightly less admiring than Whitehead: "Plato is boring."

KARL MARX (1818–1883)
FRIEDRICH ENGELS (1820–1895)

Karl Marx and Friedrich Engels were both born into wealthy, middle-class families, in the political instability of nineteenth-century Prussia (present-day Germany). Marx was encouraged by his parents to become a lawyer, Engels to take up the family textiles business, but both became distracted by Hegel, and interested in how his dialectical method intersected with social reformation and justice projects. Separately, they became involved in revolutionary movements, and subjected to police scrutiny. They traveled widely (to avoid arrest)—and their paths crossed, and minds met, in Paris in 1843—and again in London and Brussels, and variously over Europe. In 1847, they coauthored *The Communist Manifesto* (originally intended as a statement of purpose for the revolutionary group, the League of the Just). After the Prussian *coup d'état* of 1849, they moved to London where Engels funded Marx's work on *Das Kapital* (*Capital*, 1867) which laid out Marx's theory of how the capitalist economy functions while exploiting the proletariat. Both remained under police surveillance, and in London, until their deaths.

AUDRE LORDE (1934–1992)

Audre Lorde, born to immigrant parents from the West Indies, grew up in Harlem, New York City, in the fallout from the Great Depression. At an early age, she found comfort in poetry, and her later philosophical thoughts find clear and powerful expression in her poems. These works, and her essays (like those collected in the pivotal text *Sister Outsider*, 1984), deal with injustices of racism, sexism, ableism, classism, and homophobia. She is widely known for her work on intersectional feminism and her critiques of white feminism for relying on the oppressive methods and concepts of patriarchal society. In her address to a conference celebrating the thirtieth anniversary of Simone de Beauvoir's *The Second Sex* (1949), she famously stated, "the master's tools will never dismantle the master's house. They may allow us temporarily to beat him at his own game, but they will never enable us to bring about genuine change. And this fact is only threatening to those women who still define the master's house as their only source of support."

CAROLE PATEMAN (1940–)

The British feminist and political theorist Carole Pateman is perhaps best known for her 1988 book *The Sexual Contract*, in which she examines the "missing half of the story" of the concept of the social contract. She describes how the notion of the social contract, developed by Hobbes, Locke, and Rousseau, glosses over the rights it accords to men over women, and justifies a patriarchal society. She has also written on the "settler contract," which examines the concept of *terra nullius* used by colonialists to justify colonization on the grounds that they were taking control of "empty territory." Her work has heavily influenced the Jamaican-American philosopher Charles W. Mills, whose early research focused on ideology and Marxist theory before shifting to an examination of race and white supremacy. Mills's book *The Racial Contract* (1997) continues Pateman's project and demonstrates how, alongside gender, social contract theorists gloss over race—and in doing so, obscure the white supremacist political system that created the modern world. In addition to their own works, Pateman and Mills coauthored *Contract and Domination* (2007).

THE SOCIAL CONTRACT

THE MAIN CONCEPT | Some people think that all humans are naturally equal and free. But if that's the case, how can we be subject to the political authority of the state and its laws? This was the central question posed by the philosophers Thomas Hobbes and John Locke in the seventeenth century. Questioning the supposedly divine right of monarchs, and believing in the natural freedom and equality of humans, these thinkers set out to imagine a time before the state and civil society existed, as a way to both explain and justify political authority over naturally free and equal people. In *Leviathan* (1651), Hobbes described life in this "state of nature" as "nasty, brutish, and short." Without society, there are no laws, and no morality. Scarcity of resources leads to a "war of all against all," and neither art, nor culture, nor industry are possible. In his *Second Treatise on Government* (1689), Locke proposed that natural abundance eventually gives way to scarcity, and without an impartial judge to help adjudicate over this "law of nature," competition leads to conflict and strife. So how can humans live peacefully together? By reasoning that it is better to give up some of their natural freedom and equality and enter into a "social contract"—mutually consenting to live under shared laws, governed by a sovereign.

DRILL DOWN | Do contracts really promote freedom? Jean-Jacques Rousseau wasn't so sure. In the *Origin of Inequality* (1755), he argued that civil society could be a far worse place to live than as "noble savages" in the state of nature, where humans are naturally peaceful and solitary. Forming society through the mutual consent of the social contract risked reinforcing existing inequalities and exploitation. How could consent be mutual if one of the contractors was considerably stronger, or richer, than the other? Later, in *The Social Contract* (1762), Rousseau introduced the notion of the "general will," which represents the interests of the citizens as a whole. Only when individual interests and the general will are aligned can social contracts be compatible with freedom.

SWITCH UP | *Who gets to consent to the social contract? Carole Pateman, Charles W. Mills, and Stacy Clifford Simplican have separately demonstrated the various ways in which people have been systematically excluded from the pool of people considered able to give their consent to political authority—resulting from factors such as gender, race, and disability. Yet such exploitation, they point out, has also been central to the development of civil society.*

UTILITARIANISM

THE MAIN CONCEPT | Suppose you bake a delicious cake and plan on eating it all yourself. If I steal it from you and share it with ten others who really love cake, then according to utilitarianism, my action, and not yours, may be the morally right one. Utilitarians argue that the morally right action is the one that produces the most good, or "utility," even if such an action violates moral norms, or has negative consequences. This deceptively simple claim is made up of at least three commitments. First, that the consequences of an action determine whether it's right or wrong (consequentialism). Second, that what is good is happiness—pleasure and the absence of pain (hedonism). Third, that merely good consequences aren't sufficient for an action to be the right one; they must be the best possible consequences for the greatest number of people (maximization). In the eighteenth century, the philosopher Jeremy Bentham developed a "hedonic calculus" to measure and compare the happiness produced by different actions, based on metrics like duration, intensity, and "propinquity." His student John Stuart Mill then shifted the focus from the consequences of actions (act utilitarianism) to the consequences of rules (rule utilitarianism). For Mill, stealing the cake would be wrong regardless of how many cake-lovers it fed because rules that permit stealing would not produce "the greatest happiness for the greatest number."

DRILL DOWN | Imagine seeing a runaway trolley hurtling toward a fork in some train tracks. Beyond the junction lie five people who will be killed if the trolley continues on its path. But if you pull a nearby lever, you can change its trajectory onto the other branch where only one person lies unconscious. What should you do? Is it right to sacrifice one person to save five? The "trolley problem" was first posed by Philippa Foot to test our intuitions about whether or not it's morally right to sacrifice one person to save many. It has since spawned a host of variations, as well as inspiring a new field called experimental philosophy—and even a subfield known as trolleyology.

SWITCH UP | *Are there some acts you think are never, ever morally permissible? If so, utilitarianism probably isn't the theory for you. As British philosophers Elizabeth Anscombe and Bernard Williams have argued, under utilitarianism, no act is unthinkable. An agent can consider even the most horrific action, like the murder of children, as long as the results generate good outcomes for sufficient people.*

DOING YOUR DUTY
Page 22
THE VIRTUOUS PERSON
Page 26
EATING ANIMALS
Page 64

DOING YOUR DUTY

THE MAIN CONCEPT | Deriving from the Greek word *deon* (duty), deontology argues that morally right actions conform to moral rules (maxims) that generate duties to act in particular ways. It's not the consequences of your actions that matter—it's doing your duty. Sometimes doing the right thing will involve actions that have foreseeably bad consequences. Telling the truth, for instance, may end up causing harm. And sometimes good consequences aren't realizable because the actions producing them violate moral rules. (Killing the innocent is forbidden, no matter how many lives it could save.) In religious ethics, the source of "moral law" is God's will. But for the eighteenth-century German philosopher Immanuel Kant, moral rules could also derive from reason. Kant believed actions are right insofar as they conform to maxims that moral agents could will to become "universal law." Such maxims, he thought, must also coincide with the principle that we should treat others as ends in themselves, rather than as means to ends. So, for example, "Break your promises" cannot be a moral maxim because if everyone broke their promises, the very idea of "promising" would be undermined. And "Deceive people to get ahead" can't be one either, since it figures people as "means rather than ends." These guiding principles are part of what Kant called "the categorical imperative."

DRILL DOWN | Suppose someone came knocking at your door seeking to harm your housemate. Should you violate the moral duty not to lie in order to prevent the consequence of their being harmed? Controversially, Kant thought you shouldn't. This is because a moral maxim that permits lying could not rationally be made universal without significantly undermining our ability to live peaceably or even communicate effectively with each other. This highlights one problem with deontology: sometimes our duties (not to lie; to keep a friend safe from easily preventable harm) will conflict with each other.

SWITCH UP | *American ethicist Virginia Held thinks that deontology relies on the false assumption that our moral obligations can be captured by abstract, impersonal principles. It fails to acknowledge the role of feelings in arriving at moral judgments. For this reason, Held and others argue for an ethic of care, which prioritizes caring relationships as a source of moral duty.*

UTILITARIANISM
Page 20

THE VIRTUOUS PERSON
Page 26

MORAL REALISM
Page 42

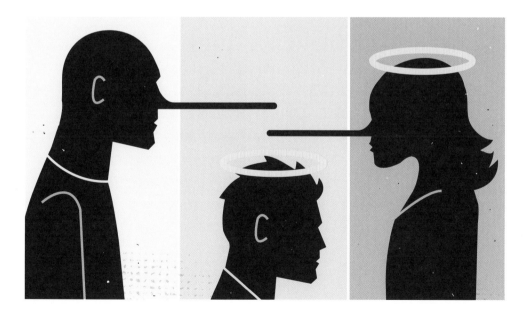

CLIMATE CHANGE

THE MAIN CONCEPT | Climate change is one of the twenty-first century's greatest challenges. As governments and scientists seek technological solutions to problems such as greenhouse gas emissions and rising sea levels, philosophers insist that climate change is an ethical and political problem—one that may fundamentally challenge our existing values and principles. Political theorist Catriona McKinnon argues that, despite the uncertainty and complexity of tracing climate impacts and framing potential solutions, humanity should adopt a "strong precautionary principle" to prevent the most serious harms from being imposed on future generations. Even if this imposes significant costs, our duties of justice, as well as the shame we should feel at causing such enormous harms, should motivate us to act. Indigenous-American and American philosophers like Kyle Whyte and Chris Cuomo press a further question: what do we owe those current generations whose cultures, practices, and very existence are threatened by climate change, against background conditions of exploitation and dispossession? The environmental ethicist Dale Jamieson suggests that the sheer scale of this issue has disrupted our usual ways of identifying harms and attributing appropriate responsibility for them.

DRILL DOWN | Indigenous and poor communities contribute least to climate change but they are most vulnerable to its harms. Studies by Robert Figueroa and Deborah McGregor in the US have demonstrated that for adaptation and mitigation efforts to be fair, indigenous communities must be consulted as experts in the observation and prediction of catastrophic climate events. In 2004, for example, the Moken people of Thailand were left largely unharmed by the tsunami that left more than 100,000 others dead because they observed signs of an impending "wave that eats people" and headed for high forest ground. And as US philosophy professor Patricia Glazebrook points out, it is often indigenous and local women who are most burdened by environmental harm, yet most expert at preventing it.

SWITCH UP | *Despite the dire threat that climate change poses to humans, many environmental philosophers criticize the human-centric nature of moral reflection. Some, like the Norwegian philosopher Arne Næss, have argued for the inherent moral value of all living beings, including plant life, while others believe we owe moral consideration to ecosystems and even things like mountains, rivers, and lakes.*

THE VIRTUOUS PERSON

THE MAIN CONCEPT | What does it mean to be a good, or virtuous, person? Why does it matter? To be virtuous is to possess a set of character traits—virtues (in the Greek, *arete*)—practiced for the right sorts of reasons and achieved by the cultivation of good moral habits. You might be someone who tells the truth, but to have the virtue of honesty you must tell the truth habitually and out of respect for the truth itself. For Aristotle and contemporary "virtue ethicists" like Rosalind Hursthouse, ethics is less about particular acts or duties, and more about good character measured in virtues and vices. The goal of life (*telos*) is to live well (*eudaimonia*). Whatever else humans seek—good health, reputation, or wealth—achieving *eudaimonia* is our highest goal. We must use rationality to act in line with what virtue demands. So, a truly virtuous person exercises practical wisdom (*phronesis*). Being honest doesn't necessarily mean bluntly telling your friends things they might not want to hear, and sometimes the bravest action might be retreat. Being virtuous requires judiciously knowing the right way to respond, to the right degree, in the right context. Without that, virtues become vicious: bravery becomes arrogance, and honesty becomes tactlessness.

SWITCH UP | *In the 1980s, Amartya Sen and Martha Nussbaum used virtue ethics to develop the "capabilities approach," a theoretical framework that has come to underpin the United Nation's Human Development Index (HDI). This measures countries' progress in terms of their citizens' freedoms to pursue meaningful activities across various domains of important human experience, like family, work, and self-respect, as an alternative to purely economic measures.*

DOING YOUR DUTY
Page 22
CULTURES OF VIOLENCE
Page 56
HYLOMORPHISM
Page 120

DRILL DOWN | Comparing and contrasting philosophical traditions from different cultures can illuminate aspects of our ethical thinking across generations and geographical distance. Recently, philosophers such as Michael Puett and Jiyuan Yu have demonstrated parallels between Aristotle's version of virtue ethics and Confucianism. In *The Ethics of Confucius and Aristotle* (2007), Yu explored how *eudaimonia* and *arete* are mirrored in the Confucian concepts of *dao* (human flourishing) and *de* (virtue and its development). But there are key differences, too. While Aristotle's ethics focuses more on the individual as the locus of *eudaimonia*, the Confucian idea of the good life considers family to be essential to cultivating important virtues like respect and honor.

PRIVATE PROPERTY

THE MAIN CONCEPT | How do we come to own things? Are our claims to private ownership justified? Philosophers have distinguished between common property that can be used by anyone in society (public walkways or land for grazing animals), collective property that can be used according to rules set by particular communities, and private property, where objects are used according to rules set by the individuals (or families or businesses) who are said to own it. In the seventeenth century, John Locke offered an influential argument for private property. For him, private property claims arose naturally from the fact that we own our own bodies and labor. By "mixing" our labor with the resources found in the natural world (land, water, timber, and so on), we come to own those things that we make, excluding others from potential ownership claims, just as long as we leave "enough and as good" for others. However, the political theorist Barbara Arneil and others have shown that Locke's argument was heavily influenced by his involvement in the English colonization of America. Since Locke—along with his fellow colonists—falsely perceived Indigenous Americans to be merely inhabiting, rather than productively using, American land, his argument was designed to block any claim to "first occupancy" that might have justified limitations on English settlement and Amerindian displacement.

DRILL DOWN | Karl Marx argued that in capitalist societies, workers exchange their productive labor for wages, not ownership. As a result, they become alienated from what they make. Institutions of private property are, therefore, a tool for the exploitation of the common people in favor of the wealthy, who stockpile money—one form of capital—as a means of acquiring social power. While under socialism we will still have private property in many things, Marx believed that the institution of private property would eventually be discarded as society progressed toward a system of large-scale cooperative labor aimed at promoting the common good. Most products would be held as common property and distributed "to each according to his needs."

SWITCH UP | *Do we own our own bodies? Should we, for example, be able to sell our bodies to offer sexual services to others? While some argue that sex work is always exploitative, social scientist Kamala Kempadoo argues that this kind of work should be understood as labor performed by marginalized people, in parallel with work carried out in other physically demanding arenas, such as agriculture and industry.*

WHITE SUPREMACY

THE MAIN CONCEPT | Although now commonly associated with groups such as the Ku Klux Klan, "white supremacy" is in fact an old term historically used by governments to pick out a pervasive and consequential political phenomenon. Jamaican-American philosopher Charles W. Mills argues that white supremacy is a political system—like feudalism or capitalism—that has "made the modern world"; 400 years of European colonialism and imperialism have produced a system in which "race" was invented to ensure that whites were systematically advantaged over nonwhites. Contemporary wealth in European ex-empires (Britain, France, and Portugal) and their ex-colonies (Australia, Canada, and Brazil) was generated by the exploitation and eradication of non-Europeans via the transatlantic slave trade and the genocide of indigenous peoples across all continents. Some claim that changes to the law resulting from civil rights and anti-colonial independence movements heralded an end to racist political structures, and even racism itself. Others believe that racism exists mainly in hate speech, bad attitudes, and even unconscious bias. But "critical philosophers of race," like Mills, argue that this reading severs the connection between those attitudes and the histories that generated them, while obscuring the role that enduring social and political white supremacist institutions play in making racism a contemporary problem.

DRILL DOWN | Liberal societies promote the belief that the best response to histories of racism is racial color-blindness—if we don't "see" color, then we won't reproduce racism. However, thinkers such as José Medina and Sara Ahmed point out that not seeing color often leads to not seeing racism, or the ways people of color are harmed by living in societies built on white supremacy. Fostering active ignorance about racism's effects and origins actually reproduces racism, promoting a social fiction that blocks the honest interrogation of well-documented social phenomena. To deny the significance of race and the existence of racism, given the overwhelming evidence to the contrary, is what Afro-Jewish philosopher Lewis Gordon labels an act of "bad faith."

SWITCH UP | *In discussions of racism, the US feminist theorist bell hooks (see page 51) chooses the phrase "white supremacy" over "racism," arguing that this shifts the focus away from white people and their attitudes, to political processes like colonization and capitalism. She also uses "white supremacist capitalist patriarchy" to describe the ways in which "systems of domination"—race, class, gender—interlock and are experienced simultaneously.*

IGNORANCE
Page 90

STANDPOINT THEORY
Page 104

NATURAL KINDS
Page 136

JUSTICE

THE MAIN CONCEPT | What does justice demand? The basic idea is that people should "get what they deserve," whether in a court of law (criminals and victims), in broader society (the rich and the poor), or on the global stage (neocolonial powers and the countries they've exploited). But what exactly do people deserve? And what principles can we use to ensure that justice is served, and in a way we might all find reasonable? Anglo-American political philosophy has long been dominated by debates about distributive justice: deciding which principles should determine how goods, opportunities, resources, rights, and freedoms are shared out between the members of a society, or even between different societies. In *A Theory of Justice* (1971), John Rawls imagined which principles of justice people would agree to if they were unaware of their position in society and other crucial facts about themselves. He theorized that they would prioritize equality and liberty, and would only accept inequalities if they were required to create the greatest benefit to the least well-off in society (the "difference principle"). His colleague Robert Nozick responded in *Anarchy, State and Utopia* (1974) by suggesting that if people freely did what they wanted with their talents or other resources, this would produce inequalities that would not necessarily benefit the worst-off, but that would be justifiable given the required respect for people's individual freedoms.

DRILL DOWN | The American political theorist Iris Marion Young argued that the distributive justice paradigm fails to capture important features of public appeals to justice made by women, people of color, indigenous peoples, and gay and lesbian civil rights movements. These groups are often excluded from political practices of collective evaluation and decision-making about institutional organization and public policy, and so lack political representation or power. These exclusions constitute injustices, which Young insisted require philosophical analysis. She defined injustice in terms of "five faces" of oppression: exploitation, marginalization, powerlessness, cultural imperialism, and violence. Justice, through the eradication of its opposite, injustice, can only be achieved via a "politics of recognition"—acknowledging different groups' experiences and political needs.

CLIMATE CHANGE
Page 24
INTERSECTIONALITY
Page 34
EPISTEMIC OPPRESSION
Page 100

SWITCH UP | *Justice in the legal–juridical sense is often understood as corrective or retributive—correcting criminals for their wrongdoing via means of retribution such as fines or imprisonment. The American activist and scholar Angela Davis argues wholesale against prison as a means to justice. She believes that in an age of racist mass incarceration, the abolishment of prisons is a central requirement for the achievement of justice in a democratic society.*

INTERSECTIONALITY

THE MAIN CONCEPT | Discussions around oppression tend to focus on a single dimension. Gender, for instance. Or class. Historically, women's suffrage movements focused exclusively on how women are disenfranchised on the basis of gender, while civil and workers' rights movements prioritized race and class respectively. In response, black, indigenous, Chicana, and Asian women have insisted that such single-issue framing fails to serve those who are harmed by sexism, racism, and classism all at once (as well as by imperialism, dis/ableism, heterosexism, and cissexism). In addition, people can be both oppressed and oppressors—many white suffragettes, for example, actively sought to deny black women the vote. Intersectionality is a way of thinking about social inequality that acknowledges that our position in society results from complex, mutually reinforcing factors. In the mid-twentieth century, writers such as Francis Beale and Deborah King, alongside the black feminist lesbian cooperative the Combahee River Collective, emphasized the importance of thinking multidimensionally about oppression, rooted in the lived experiences of those most disadvantaged by it. In the 1990s, Kimberlé Crenshaw popularized the term "intersectionality," highlighting the US legal system's failure to recognize wrongdoing against black women who experienced racialized sexism and gendered racism.

DRILL DOWN | In their 2016 book *Intersectionality*, Patricia Hill Collins and Sirma Bilge discussed how critics of intersectionality tend to focus on the way that it seems to promote a form of "identity politics"—that acknowledging people's various identities (black, female, disabled, queer) somehow draws attention away from the social and political structures that are the "real" sources of injustice. Critics also claim that intersectional analysis erases the importance of class as a primary source of oppression. However, it is worth questioning the extent to which such objections are based on an accurate and even charitable understanding of the long history of work on intersectionality and related concepts.

SWITCH UP | *Audre Lorde writes that, as a black, disabled, feminist lesbian, constantly being encouraged to "eclipse or deny" the totality of who she is in favor of selecting some singular aspect of herself to represent her identity is a "destructive" way to live. Only by allowing power to flow "freely between . . . different selves" and by reinterpreting "deviance" as "difference" can she live freely.*

WHITE SUPREMACY
Page 30

EPISTEMIC OPPRESSION
Page 100

STANDPOINT THEORY
Page 104

DISABILITY

THE MAIN CONCEPT | Philosophers have historically had a complicated relationship with disability. It has been either largely absent from philosophical inquiries, or introduced as a foil to think about other topics. For example, John Rawls (see page 32) explicitly instructed his readers not to think about disability when framing principles of justice lest it arouse "pity and anxiety." When disability has been addressed directly, questions have focused on what obligations societies have to redistribute resources to disabled people. Some philosophers even ask whether there's a moral obligation to "eradicate" disability if, as some assume, disabled lives are only ever characterized by suffering. Disability is philosophically interesting, and ideas about ability have deep and consequential roots in philosophy. In ethics, rationality and other mental and physical capacities are often given as requirements for personhood, moral agency, or even basic moral consideration. In social and political philosophy, racist and sexist theories about natural subordination often turn on the claim that certain individuals lack "normal" capacities and so can only live well under the governance of husbands, masters, or imperial rulers. Mainstream philosophy, therefore, has largely evolved without reference to the lives, experiences, or philosophical thinking of disabled people.

DRILL DOWN | "Critical disability studies" has led the way in shifting understanding of disability from being something solely "in the body" to something socially constructed. The British "social model of disability" contends that disability results from prejudicial biases, attitudes, structures, and systems that make life harder for those with "impairments," whether physical, psychological, or cognitive (being paraplegic, being dyspraxic, or being schizophrenic, for example). Recent philosophical work interrogates this new paradigm. Philosopher Shelley Tremain argues that ideas about what constitutes impairment are socially constructed; English philosopher Elizabeth Barnes states that disability is best understood as that cluster of experiences and issues around which disability rights activists have tried to promote justice; and Susan Wendell, author of *The Rejected Body* (1996), argues that chronic illness ought to be considered a form of disability.

SWITCH UP | *Bioethics asks philosophical questions about the ethics of clinical practice and medical policy. It has been criticized by disability activists and scholars for its exclusion of critical disability perspectives. Anita Ho has shown that even in current bioethics textbooks, disability is not taken seriously as a critical perspective. What consequences might this have for disabled and chronically ill patients who encounter bioethics students as doctors?*

CONSERVATISM

THE MAIN CONCEPT | Sometimes the pace with which people seek to reform social institutions and traditions can seem overwhelming. According to some sets of political beliefs, the right way to approach the business of government is to preserve the wisdom built up through tried-and-tested practices. Conservatism is a right-wing political ideology characterized by a commitment to traditional values and social institutions, such as religion, aristocracy, and the monarchy. Twenty-first-century conservatism incorporates a concern for the exercise of freedoms, particularly in relation to free markets, with varying degrees of commitment to social freedoms at odds with long-standing public ideas about morality (about LBGTQ+ rights, for example). Conservatives are skeptical of radical reform. They're aware of the limits of human rationality, and doubt that any single generation is capable of improving institutions that have developed and adapted over centuries. The classical texts of early conservative thought were written by the Irish philosopher and statesman Edmund Burke. In his *Reflections on the Revolution in France* (1790), Burke condemned the revolutionists as "a swinish multitude," performing violent, destructive actions on the basis of abstract ideology, which (given the limitations of human rationality) couldn't possibly capture the complexity of the sociopolitical situation.

DRILL DOWN | Political conservatives are faced with a conceptual quandary. How long does something have to exist for it to become a "traditional" institution? How do traditions emerge in the first place? And how do they become tried and tested? What about traditions that we would now consider immoral? Answers to these questions will depend on how you understand tradition—and a lot of intellectual work has gone into discussing this. According to Burke, the emergence of institutions is an organic process. Rather than a revolutionary shift in societal currents, changes can be introduced gently, rather than in "the blind and furious spirit of innovation" (as the British Prime Minister Benjamin Disraeli once put it).

THE SOCIAL CONTRACT
Page 18
THE STANDARD OF TASTE
Page 72
IGNORANCE
Page 90

SWITCH UP | *Is conservatism a genuine philosophical position? Some philosophers think it's a matter of faith—of putting trust in traditional organizations—rather than the support of any specific theoretical model. As such, certain thinkers, like Gordon Graham, classify conservatism as a "non-ideology." But could it be that this dismissal is itself ideologically motivated?*

QUEER THEORY

THE MAIN CONCEPT | To call someone "queer" originally meant that they were strange or different, and it was often used as a slur against people falling under the LGBTQ+ umbrella. However, in the 1980s, LGBTQ+ communities began to reclaim the term as a neutral, or positive, way to describe themselves. "Queer" is now sometimes used as a word for anyone who is not heterosexual (sexually attracted to the "opposite" sex) or cisgender (people whose gender identity aligns with the sex they were assigned at birth). Queer theory tends to see "queer" as a verb: something people do rather than something that people are. Queer theory is thus defined as a resistance to "the normal" rather than resistance to heterosexuality. Activist-academic Meg-John Barker argues that queer theory challenges a trio of related assumptions. First, sexual identity is fixed from birth. Scientific evidence shows that sexual identity changes as we mature and come to better understand our sexuality. The second assumption is that sexuality is binary (straight or gay), based on binary attraction to men or women. But neither sexuality nor gender are universally experienced as binary. They are often strongly informed by cultural contexts. Third, queer theory challenges the assumption that sexual attractions and practices can be divided into "normal" or "abnormal."

DRILL DOWN | American poet and essayist Adrienne Rich argues that women are coerced into "compulsory heterosexuality" and patriarchal gender norms; they gain privilege and status from conformity and experience loss or punishment if they choose to deviate. Such punishments—from social stigma to legal prohibitions—would not be necessary if heterosexuality was as natural as it claims to be. Judith Butler argues that gender is not essential, natural, or stable, but "performative," based merely on our behavior or expressions (our choice of clothing, how we walk, how we talk). In other words, society offers us scripts for what it is to be a man or a woman.

SWITCH UP | *Transgender philosopher Talia Mae Bettcher argues that respect for "first person authority" (FPA) (the ability to make a statement about one's own attitudes or states without external justification) distinguishes trans-exclusive from trans-inclusive social contexts. FPA is key to understanding and combating forms of transphobia or cissexism such as misgendering (denying someone's gender identity).*

MORAL REALISM

THE MAIN CONCEPT | What are we doing when we make moral claims like "Killing the innocent is wrong" or "Being charitable is good"? Some believe that we are trying to make statements about how the world is, and not just our feelings about it. Moral realists believe that when we make moral claims, we are trying to make statements about facts and properties that exist independently of our opinions about them, and that such statements can be true or false. Plato believed that moral properties such as goodness and justice—as well as nonmoral properties such as redness and squareness—were really existing entities. He labeled these "Forms." Plato believed that when we encounter a red cube, we encounter a physical manifestation of the Forms of redness and squareness. Similarly, witnessing an act of charity and judging it to be good is like claiming that charity manifests the Form of goodness. Some contemporary moral realists, such as moral naturalists, take a much more scientific approach, believing that we can discover moral facts using scientific methods, such as observation. Others disagree, denying that we are able to observe moral properties directly in the world, unlike "natural" properties like roundness or redness. For them, moral properties such as goodness are instead detected in similar ways to complex natural properties such as healthiness.

DRILL DOWN | Moral non-cognitivism denies that moral claims are claims about the world. Instead, they are simply complicated expressions of feeling or approval. In *Language, Truth, and Logic* (1936), A. J. Ayer argued that the statement "Murder is wrong" is just a complex way of saying, "Boo, murder!" On the other hand, error theorists like J. L. Mackie believe that moral claims are attempts to say something true about the world, but that they fail miserably. If moral facts and properties did exist, they'd be too peculiar—metaphysically speaking—for us to be able to detect them, so to be able to say true or false things about them. Our moral claims are, as such, made in error.

SWITCH UP | *If moral realism is false, it's easy to be left with an uneasy sense that morality boils down to a doctrine of anything goes, where moral judgments merely reflect our individual or social preferences or habits. If so, then what's the point of making moral judgments at all? And how is moral progress, either in ourselves or across societies, possible?*

CULTURAL RELATIVISM
Page 74

SOCIAL ONTOLOGY
Page 134

NATURAL KINDS
Page 136

"Popular culture is one of the sites where this struggle for and against a culture of the powerful is engaged: it is also the stake to be won or lost in that struggle."

STUART HALL,
CULTURAL STUDIES 1983: A THEORETICAL HISTORY

2

CULTURE

INTRODUCTION

The word "culture" is polyvalent—it means different things. It can be used as a verb— one can culture cells, for example—while used as a noun it describes things as varied as pieces of art or music, practices of creative expression, and even the social groups associated with them. In this chapter, we are going to follow suit and cover the broadest range of philosophical topics relating to culture, rather than sticking to a single definition.

"The Arts"

In the Western intellectual tradition, philosophers have consistently taken an interest in The Arts—in literature, music, and visual arts such as painting and sculpture. Often, philosophical works are themselves considered artworks, too—Plato's dialogues and Simone de Beauvoir's novels, for example.

Some of the topics that follow examine philosophical debates about culture in this narrower sense: What is an artwork, exactly? Do artworks have to be acknowledged as such by the so-called Art World? What is it that we find disturbing about fakes and forgeries? How do we explain our genuine emotional engagement with fictional characters? In Euro-American philosophy, these questions normally fall within the sphere of aesthetics, the subdiscipline that examines issues to do with beauty and taste, focusing on the engagement of the senses and the imagination.

The culture of a place

Culture also picks out systems of knowledge and social practices. So, in talking about American culture, you might include—alongside the output of American artists—apple pie, Republican democracy, diners, and baseball; the culture of the place. Thinking about culture like this prompts different kinds of philosophical debate. What happens when you imitate—or appropriate—the attitudes or styles of other societies? And, not unrelatedly, is morality universal ("pan-cultural"), or might different societies have relativized moralities specific to their own culture?

Food and culinary traditions fall within both the broad and narrow ambit of culture. Encounters to do with taste are the subject of aesthetic appreciation—take wine connoisseurs, for instance. But the dietary habits of social groups are also the focus of moral and political attention. In some parts of the world, vegetarianism and veganism are widespread, and in others, meat-eating is more common. Ethical attitudes toward food vary considerably; even within meat-eating societies there are various implicit rules that dictate which meats can and can't be eaten—is it okay to eat cow, or dog, or horse meat?

Culturing culture

Culture also means to "encourage" or "cultivate"—and it's fair to say that people like to culture culture. On the whole, we consider culture (meaning, narrowly, The Arts) to be a good thing, a positive feature of societies. However, there are elements of culture that people try to discourage or restrict. Certain artifacts are subject to censorship. As we'll see, this includes things like pornography, and specific sorts of humor. Are there any kinds of jokes that should be banned? And how does the concept of free speech intersect with all these issues?

Philosophical culture

However the word "culture" is understood, philosophers are very much a part of it—and yet their work doesn't always acknowledge this fact. In creating their metaphysical systems and moral theories, scholars in the European and American traditions are prone to try to assume a position outside culture, the so-called "view from nowhere." From Plato to Descartes to Hume and Kant, philosophers have taken supposedly objective stances. They like to make universal claims, whether about the concept of beauty, or the notion of the "good."

If nothing else, this chapter should give you a sense that these philosophers and their theories are very much products of particular times and places—and that it pays to take their historical and political backgrounds into account. As the American anthropologist Clifford Geertz put it: it's culture all the way down!

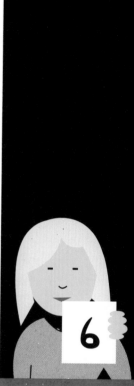

TIMELINE

ICONOCLASM

Rome falls and Byzantium and the Eastern Church rise to power. Emperor Leo III inaugurates a period known as Byzantine iconoclasm, during which the arts become the subject of intense religious censorship. This period sees widescale destruction of religious images on moral grounds.

RENAISSANCE THINKING

After the Islamic Golden Age, Europe is taken by the so-called Renaissance spirit—the "rebirth" of ancient philosophy. It begins in the Italian city-states, where powerful political dynasties sponsor thinkers to develop the kinds of mathematical theories of art, literature, and beauty first found in Greek and Roman thought.

400 BCE — **700 CE** — **1100** — **1300**

ANCIENT PHILOSOPHY

Despite long-running conflict between Greece and the Persian Empire, Athens is prosperous and detached enough to become a cultural capital. Here, Socrates and Diotima discuss the nature of beauty, while Plato articulates the forms of "acceptable" culture. Their theories go on to shape the views of Aristotle and Saint Augustine.

IBN RUSHD

The Arabic philosopher Ibn Rushd (Averroes) is instrumental in reviving interest in Classical Greek thinking in Europe, particularly that of Aristotle. He argues for the importance of philosophy as well as theology, and offers influential commentaries on Aristotle's *Poetics*.

MODERNISM

Modernism is born, in response to the growth of "modern" industrial societies and the pervasive feeling that Enlightenment values have become outdated. New forms of literature (abstract art and stream-of-consciousness novels) are created, and new forms of philosophy emerge to discuss them.

POPULAR CULTURE

The start of a new century sees a burgeoning of philosophical interest in popular culture and cultural appropriation, prompted by the work of bell hooks and others. Within analytic philosophy, a lot of aesthetic discussion is "neo-Aristotelian"; aestheticians look at how fictions prompt or hinder ethical development.

1600   **1800**   **1900**   **2000**

IMPERIAL EUROPE

Europe grows wealthy off the colonization of the Americas, and the transatlantic slave trade. This financial upturn increases both philosophical and cultural output. Funded by rich backers, Francis Bacon and Blaise Pascal write treatises on music and discourses on beauty.

POSTMODERNISM

Civil rights movements generate increased awareness of racist and patriarchal cultural trends. Postmodernism develops in response to the confident declamations of the modernist movement, with Judith Butler and Jacques Derrida targeting cultural norms and notions of objective reality and aesthetics.

BIOGRAPHIES

SOCRATES (c. 470–399 BCE)

Socrates was born in Alopeke in what is now
Greece, and wrote no texts of his own—but
we know a good deal of his life through the
accounts of his student Plato. He is famous for
his distinctive form of dialogic argument, by
which groups of interlocutors are encouraged
to clarify ideas through a series of well-placed
questions. In Plato's *Symposium* (385–370 BCE)
we also learn about Socrates's views on love and
beauty—developed in conversation with the
priestess Diotima of Mantinea. A central strand
in Socratic thought is that love is an attitude that
seeks out beauty—and that what is truly beautiful
is necessarily good—thus love strives always
upward, toward goodness. This account results
in the so-called "ladder of love": one can start
by loving someone—as Socrates loved his student
Alcibiades—erotically. Erotic love can then shift
to love of a spiritual nature, which in turn may
shift to love of the abstract idea of beauty (the
final rung on the ladder). Socrates was ever one
to put theory into practice, and while married to
the long-suffering Xanthippe, enjoyed a number
of erotic, homosexual relationships with his
friends and associates.

IMMANUEL KANT (1724–1804)

The German philosopher Immanuel Kant was
a dour, controlling figure, who spent most of
his life in the small town of Königsberg, where
he was born. While the man himself traveled
rarely, his ideas have permeated European and
American philosophy. His *Critique of Judgment*
(1790) is one of the foundational texts for
present-day discussions of aesthetics; it
comprises an extended meditation on the nature
of art, truth, and beauty—and examines how
these concepts intersect with the subjects of
his earlier two *Critiques* (on *Pure Reason* and
Practical Reason—1781 and 1788). In the third
Critique, Kant offers a detailed definition of
beauty—describing the ideas that underpin
our current judgments of taste. The level of
precision that he applied to conceptual analysis
also extended into his everyday life; he was
notorious for his rigorous approach to cultural
appreciation, famously laying out rules for
"good dining" in his fastidious *Anthropology
from a Pragmatic Point of View* (1798). His dinner
parties were known for being supremely well
ordered—if not particularly fun.

IRIS MURDOCH (1919–1999)

It is common in the twentieth-century French and German traditions to find figures known both as philosophers and novelists. The Irish author Jean Iris Murdoch is noteworthy for being just one of a handful British-based thinkers who moved comfortably between these spheres, writing both fiction and academic philosophy. Her novels—among them, *Under the Net*, *The Sandcastle*, and *The Bell* (1954, 1957, and 1958)—are transfused with thoughts on moral philosophy and Murdoch's interest in the Aristotelian virtues. Her philosophical works, such as *The Sovereignty of Good* (1970), explicitly challenge much of the then consensus "behaviorist" view of moral philosophy and foreground the "inner life" of moral action. According to Murdoch, we should think about not just how people behave, but how they feel. In claiming this, she positioned herself alongside her contemporaries at Oxford—Elizabeth Anscombe, Mary Midgley, and Philippa Foot (the latter of whom was a one-time lover, and long-time interlocutor). Murdoch was known for her ready wit and exciting sex life, writing once that "human affairs are not serious . . . but they have to be taken seriously."

BELL HOOKS (1952–)

Gloria Jean Watkins was born in the small town of Hopkinsville in Kentucky. She took the name bell hooks in honor of her maternal grandmother, Bell Blair Hooks, and pens it with lowercase letters to emphasize her writing and ideas over her personality, and to challenge grammatical orthodoxy. hooks is known both as a philosopher and a social activist; her work investigates the concepts of race, gender, and capitalism, and the ways these perpetuate oppression. Unlike many philosophers in the European and American traditions, hooks considers works of popular culture—pop songs and mainstream blockbusters, for instance—sites of important intellectual labor as well as ideological activity. She engages with them just as much as with dry academic treatises. Born into a working-class family, and educated in a racially segregated public school, hooks is acutely aware of how certain art forms, environments, and modes of presentation exclude particular audiences. Through her theory, theoretical style, and teaching methods, she has therefore tried to develop work and teaching practices that are anti-elitist and accessible to all.

THE CATEGORY OF "ART"

THE MAIN CONCEPT | What unites Frida Kahlo's *Without Hope* and Tracey Emin's unmade bed? What links Marcel Duchamp's readymades and Barbara Hepworth's sculptures? These disparate artifacts are all considered art. But what is art exactly? Over the years, philosophers have offered a variety of competing definitions. According to the "institutionalist" definition, an art object is one that a certain group of people—described by American art critic Arthur Danto as "the Artworld"—have deemed appropriate for artistic appreciation by a public. Emin's bed is art because art critics say it is. By contrast, the "intentional–historical" definition, endorsed by aesthetician Jerrold Levinson, holds that an artwork is a "thing which has been seriously intended for regarding-as-a-work-of-art." It's the creator's intention, not the critics, which is relevant; if you've created something with the aim that it be taken as an artwork, then that's enough to make it art. Then there are the "functional" definitions, which state that art should be defined in relation to its effects on an audience (rather than focusing on artists or critics). According to the American philosopher Monroe Beardsley, an artwork is "an arrangement of conditions intended to be capable of affording an experience with marked aesthetic character." But do any of these really capture the essence of art?

DRILL DOWN | The twentieth-century aesthetician Peg Zeglin Brand encourages us to interrogate the category of art from a feminist perspective. Brand has drawn our attention to the patriarchal histories of art that have dominated Western culture, as has the art theorist Linda Nochlin. Brand points out that much artwork produced by women is ignored in the canon, and sometimes dismissed as "craftwork" rather than "artwork." Consequently, definitions of art constructed around the canon (as the institutionalist and intentional–historical are) may be structured to exclude certain artworks, like knitting, tapestry, and needlework. Her belief that we should examine the way we create definitions has achieved justified prominence in these philosophical debates.

SWITCH UP | *Is art really a category in need of a definition? The author Ellen Dissanayake suggests that we should think of art as a behavior instead—as something that people simply do. For Dissanayake, art is like talking and eating and playing. "Making special," as she puts it, is simply a feature of our multifarious human lives. As such, it can have no essential features.*

BEAUTY

THE MAIN CONCEPT | In Euro-American philosophy, the concept of beauty is heavily shaped by the German philosopher Immanuel Kant. In his *Critique of Judgment* (1790), Kant tried to work out what beauty is precisely—and what we mean when we say something is beautiful. Kant described four criteria that he believed underpin our judgments about beauty. Firstly, they are disinterested—we are not particularly interested in the beautiful object, except insofar as it is beautiful. We might take pleasure in the beauty of a sunrise, without being interested in its various elements—the sun's rays and surrounding cloud formations, for instance. Secondly and thirdly, such judgments are universal and necessary. Unlike claims about favorite flavors of ice-cream, claims about beauty are supposed to permit no disagreement. Fourthly, Kant believed that aesthetic judgments figure beautiful objects as purposive without purpose; we may judge that a painting is beautiful without being able to say exactly what it's for. Likewise, a magnolia tree may be beautiful when in bloom, and the harmony of the elements—the delicate blush of the petals and lattice of branch—may give the impression of purposive design, even if no purpose for such things can be found.

DRILL DOWN | The concept of beauty is not without its problems. Kant held that "the beautiful" is an "object of universal satisfaction"; beautiful things are beautiful for everyone. However, as Shirley Anne Tate pointed out in *Black Beauty* (2009), such views lead to the peculiar claim that all humans are supposed to "feel beauty in exactly the same way." Moreover, Tate demonstrates how such universalizing attitudes have troubling political consequences. "There are racialized aesthetics," she says, "which attempt to be universal by uniting beauty with some bodies while othering others . . ." Judgments about beauty are specific to particular historical and cultural contexts—and traditional (European) notions of beauty can exclude black bodies while focusing on white ones.

SWITCH UP | *The nineteenth-century Ceylonese-British philosopher and art historian Ananda Coomaraswamy was heavily involved in the project of examining Western standards of beauty. Following research trips in Ceylon (present-day Sri Lanka), he returned to London, where he critiqued curatorial approaches to ancient Indian art, the value and beauty of which were seen to be primarily archaeological rather than artistic. His attention to Indian art in the British context positioned it at the roots of Western art movements such as British modernism.*

DOING YOUR DUTY
Page 22
EVERYDAY AESTHETICS
Page 58
IGNORANCE
Page 90

CULTURES OF VIOLENCE

THE MAIN CONCEPT | From the *Epic of Gilgamesh* (2100 BCE) onward, artworks have represented violent actions. For almost as long, these representations have been the subject of moral debate. Sometimes, fictions seem to glamorize and normalize violence. This is a complaint often made against computer games, rap music, and popular Hollywood movies, all of which can contain highly graphic depictions of bloodshed. The framing thought here—that one may become used to certain attitudes through repeated exposure—has a long-standing pedigree. In the *Nichomachean Ethics* (350 BCE), Aristotle describes how moral virtue, or excellence of character, is borne out of habit. In the same way that tennis practice improves your tennis game, practicing courage makes you more courageous. For Aristotle, the virtues included moral or intellectual dispositions, covering attitudes like temperance, friendliness, common sense, wisdom, and understanding—all of which could be developed through repetition and performance. Friendliness is, in a sense, a muscle one has to flex. Aristotle, then, may have had an interesting take on contemporary gaming culture. Violent games may prohibit the development of virtues (temperance and friendliness). Or maybe they foster virtue, if they put us in situations where we can choose courage over cowardice. It depends on how you play them.

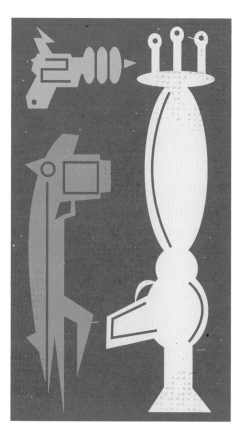

DRILL DOWN | According to Aristotle, and neo-Aristotelians like Iris Murdoch, it's impossible to separate out the ethical and emotional aspects of our characters—the two are too deeply enmeshed. He believed that we can train ourselves to be happy when we act virtuously, and feel shame when we don't. In the *Poetics* (335 BCE), he describes a system for the cultivation of virtues, and a central concept in this system is "catharsis"—roughly speaking, letting off emotional steam, often in response to fictional scenarios. You may, for instance, feel overwhelmed by melancholy and sadness; in order to purge yourself of dangerous excesses of these emotions, you should, says Aristotle, attend a tragic play and direct your melancholy toward fictional characters (rather than fellow citizens).

SWITCH UP | *C. Thi Nguyen is a philosopher currently working on the ethics of video games. Alongside games developer José Zagal, he asks important questions about the ethical norms found in massive multiplayer online games. Where, for example, do these ethical norms come from? The fictional universe or the gaming community? What concerns might there be over engaging with these norms through "avatars"—characters often created to be wildly different from their players?*

EVERYDAY AESTHETICS

THE MAIN CONCEPT | Aesthetics, the Euro-American discipline that focuses on art and art practices, typically sees art to be "fine art"—poetry, paintings, novels, and so on. However, a growing number of philosophers are encouraging us to broaden this disciplinary focus to include what they call "everyday aesthetics." They point out that our lives outside gallery spaces involve many aesthetical encounters, with things as disparate as domestic practices, interpersonal interactions, and sports like baseball. A well-crafted, sharp knife may be a subject of aesthetic appreciation. So may a football game (encompassing the cheers of fans and the smell of hotdogs). Proponents of everyday aesthetics argue that, as well as investigating these alternative sites, we should also attend to a wider range of aesthetic qualities. Kant may have been obsessed with beauty, but other people and cultures are interested in qualities like the monotonous, the gaudy, and the tranquil. Beyond Europe, such everyday aesthetic qualities have long been the focus of artistic appreciation—as in, for example, Japanese tea ceremonies. This strand of aesthetics also focuses on the openness of daily encounters; not all art exists within a frame, and framing limits the audience's phenomenological purview.

DRILL DOWN | The philosophy professor Yuriko Saito has examined art encountered in daily life as part and parcel of her critique of traditional Western modes of art appreciation. The dominant focus on beauty, and on the objects housed within galleries, is intellectually and culturally limiting. For one thing, it privileges certain types of viewing experience, reliant on certain institutions, such as major art galleries. Art appreciation is then rendered elitist and exclusive, since it is only open to those who have access to these institutions. Everyday aesthetics encourages a wider, more democratic engagement with aesthetic encounters that are more accessible—like the simple act of combing your hair, for example.

SWITCH UP | *How easy is it for us to "appreciate" the everyday aesthetic quality of the gross? When was the last time you felt inclined to reflect on the smelly contents of a dustbin or the tedium of a lengthy queue? Yuriko Saito points out how difficult it can be to relinquish the standard ways of "seeing" art and the dominant conceptions of beauty that prevail in the West.*

HUMOR

THE MAIN CONCEPT | Philosophers can suck the joy out of pretty much everything—including humor itself. Take Plato; he saw laughter as an emotion that undermines self-control and presents an obstacle to rational deliberation. "A fit of laughter," he said, "almost always produces a violent reaction." Accordingly, he advised the readers of *The Republic* (c. 380 BCE) to avoid it. He wanted all citizens to be clear-headed and emotionally undisturbed. He also considered humor and laughter to be essentially mean or malicious. This is the so-called "superiority account" of humor, also endorsed by Thomas Hobbes and René Descartes. According to this view, laughter is scornful—we laugh because we think people are foolish, because they are "self-ignorant," thinking themselves better looking or cleverer than they actually are. Humor, then, is a morally objectionable practice. When we laugh, it is always at the expense of others. Because of this, Plato thought that laughter and the humor that prompts it should be strictly regulated. His *Laws* (c. 348 BCE) present an ideal world in which "No composer of comedy, iambic or lyric verse shall be permitted to hold any citizen up to laughter, by word or gesture, with passion or otherwise."

DRILL DOWN | The eighteenth-century Irish philosopher Francis Hutcheson scoffed at the superiority account of humor. He pointed out that a sense of superiority is neither sufficient nor necessary for us to find something funny. We can feel superior to animals without laughing at them (so it's not sufficient). And we laugh at things that we do not feel superior to—we find incongruity funny, for instance (so it's not necessary). A century later, the German thinker Arthur Schopenhauer also advocated the "incongruity thesis," holding that we find humor in things that violate normal expectations: a duck wearing a bowler hat, for instance.

SWITCH UP | *The American philosopher Ted Cohen thought about jokes in terms of intimacy and community building. In* Jokes: Philosophical Thoughts on Joking Matters *(1999), he writes that "the deep satisfaction in successful joke transactions is the sense held mutually by teller and hearer that they are joined in feeling." If you find my joke funny, we've connected somehow. That's one of the reasons it feels so unsettling when a joke fails to land.*

THE ETHICS OF ART

THE MAIN CONCEPT | Traditionally, there have been two opposed philosophical positions regarding the ethical criticism of art. The first, autonomism, holds that we should evaluate art using only aesthetic standards, rather than placing artworks in categories like "moral" or "immoral." Philosophers on this side of the debate argue that, since the arts fall within an autonomous domain, we should respond only to the aesthetic qualities of an artwork. This is comparable, for example, to the way that we think that the sciences should not be subject to aesthetic standards. In other words, it doesn't matter if audiences find D. W. Griffith's movie *Birth of a Nation* (1915) morally reprehensible—the direction and story-telling can still be found impressive, or even beautiful, depending on your stylistic sensibilities. The second position is moralism, which holds that the aesthetic value of art—namely the pleasure (or displeasure) an art object elicits when appreciated aesthetically—can be reduced to its ethical value. The Russian novelist Leo Tolstoy advocated the moralist position, arguing that the proper purpose of art was not beauty or pleasure but the moral utility it could serve in our lives. According to this view, Mary Shelley's beautifully crafted sentences in *Frankenstein* (1823) are not as important as the moral message that humans should not aspire to "play God."

DRILL DOWN | The American aesthetician A. W. Eaton offers us the notion of "rough heroes." Narratives often offer us morally flawed protagonists who have no redeeming qualities, but who audiences tend to perceive as charming or sympathetic. Take Hannibal Lecter, for instance. Moralists want to construe such narratives as immoral since they "throw our sympathies to the side of sin," and create a tension between our emotional approval and our moral condemnation of a person. Implicitly, for the moralist, an immoral character is an aesthetic failure when they elicit sympathy. For Eaton, however, rough hero narratives hold particular aesthetic merits. They can make audiences feel things they are strongly disinclined to feel. Such an effect takes considerable artistry.

SWITCH UP | *The debate between moralists and autonomists focuses primarily on the narrative arts—movies, comics, and novels, for instance—but what about more abstract forms of art, such as the musical arts, which are often non-narrative? To what extent can moral considerations be brought to bear on nonrepresentational musical forms?*

THE CATEGORY OF "ART"
Page 52
CULTURES OF VIOLENCE
Page 56
FORGERIES & FAKES
Page 70
SOCIAL EPISTEMOLOGY
Page 98

EATING ANIMALS

THE MAIN CONCEPT | People in many cultures value the presence of meat products in their diets. Whether it's the British Sunday roast or Jamaican jerk chicken, eating animals plays a significant role in a wide range of dietary and culinary practices. While philosophers aren't always known for their compassion toward animals—Thomas Aquinas denied them entry to heaven, and Descartes happily carried out surgical experimentation on living creatures—they have debated the ethics of our treatment of animals, including whether we should eat them. One prominent argument against eating meat hinges on what psychologist and animal activist Richard Ryder calls "speciesism"—the claim that species membership is crucial to moral status. Utilitarian philosopher Peter Singer popularized this concept in his book *Animal Liberation* (1975). Singer follows Jeremy Bentham in arguing that a being's moral status depends on whether it is sentient (capable of suffering); if a being suffers, then it is owed moral concern. Singer argues that however meat-eaters benefit from eating meat—culturally, nutritionally, or just because they find it tasty—such benefits will never be sufficient to justify the suffering of nonhuman animals.

DRILL DOWN | Should everyone become a vegetarian? Cultural theorist Cathryn Bailey argues that demands to adopt certain dietary practices need to be contextualized. Culinary traditions can have symbolic power and the eating of nonvegetarian foodstuffs—like gefilte fish, jerk chicken, and jambalaya—may be important for community and cultural identity. It might not be appropriate to demand vegetarianism from someone whose cultural heritage involves meat-eating. Other thinkers, like Carol J. Adams, argue that cultural practices around meat-eating can be deeply enmeshed in broader sociocultural problems, such as the misogynistic language that associates women with cuts of meat ("leg man," "breast man"), or the environmental harms caused by meat-production industries.

SWITCH UP | *Can the actions of an individual have much effect on the global meat industries? This is a "collective action problem." It's clear that the combined efforts of a large number of people might have the power to effect positive change, but recognizing this draws attention to the ineffectiveness of a single person's decision-making powers. To counteract this, activists run campaigns like "Meat-Free Monday"— so everybody can act together.*

THE PARADOX OF FICTION

THE MAIN CONCEPT | The paradox of fiction rests on three main claims. The first is the thought that, for us to be moved emotionally by people or events, we must believe that those people or events actually exist. Can I really be sad about the death of my hamster, Alfred, if I discover Alfred doesn't really exist? The second is the claim that, when we engage with fiction—be it a novel, movie, or comic book—we know that the fictional characters contained within it are, in fact, not real. They don't exist. It doesn't matter how great I think Wonder Woman is—ultimately, I'm fully aware she's an imaginative fiction. The third claim—which seems undoubtedly true—is that we are sometimes moved by, and emotionally engaged with, blatantly fictional characters. I can, for instance, find myself attracted to Mr. Darcy from Jane Austen's *Pride and Prejudice*, or the heroine of Tolstoy's *Anna Karenina*. I'm sad when my favorite characters die, and happy when they triumph. These three statements sit in tension with one another; it seems that they can't all be true, which is why philosophers have tried to resolve this paradoxical situation by rejecting one or more of these claims.

DRILL DOWN | The logician Eva Schaper rejected the idea that we have to believe someone or something is real to be moved by them or it. Instead, she claims, our emotional responses depend on our assessments of described or perceived characteristics. Does the object of our attention really possess fearful or lovable or admirable qualities? Those are the focuses of our fearful, loving, admiring responses. American philosopher Kendall Walton, on the other hand, denies the third premise of the paradox of fiction; we aren't actually emotionally engaged with Mr. Darcy—we're make-believing emotional involvement (and this is why we don't run screaming from theaters when we see a scary movie monster).

CULTURES OF VIOLENCE
Page 56

THE ETHICS OF ART
Page 62

THE ONTOLOGICAL ARGUMENT
Page 142

SWITCH UP | *American metaphysician Amie Thomasson and others are interested in whether or not fictional characters actually exist. Instinctively, we would probably say "no." At the same time, there's something both appealing and insightful in the thought that certain characters take on a life of their own. Are we really sure that Sherlock Holmes and Madame Bovary aren't, in some sense, real?*

CULTURAL APPROPRIATION

THE MAIN CONCEPT | In her essay, "Eating the Other" (1992), bell hooks tells us: "Within commodity culture, ethnicity becomes spice, seasoning that can liven up the dull dish that is mainstream white culture." She's talking about cultural appropriation—the way that cultural practices or traditions are co-opted or adopted by other cultures. It's possible to appropriate objects (miniature Buddha statues), hairstyles (Rastafarian locks), or bodily decoration (Hindu and Jain bindis). It's also possible to appropriate ways of being—think of middle-class white people using African-American Vernacular English while fist-bumping their middle-class white friends. There are innumerable modes of cultural appropriation and all of them risk distorting the original culture from which the tradition is drawn. In his book *Orientalism* (1978), Edward W. Said described the way that Western society flattens the traditions of what it sees to be "the East" or "the Orient" by exoticizing them—that is, by making them superficially mysterious and otherworldly. According to Said, Middle Eastern, South Asian, and East Asian peoples are conflated into a homogenous Other, with exotic attitudes and dress, customs that are then reproduced, wholesale and uncritically, in the literature and fashions of the West.

DRILL DOWN | Some say imitation is the sincerest form of flattery. When it comes to appropriation, however, serious harms can result from the annexation of another's culture. The Cherokee scholar Adrienne Keene has demonstrated how appropriation leads to the perpetuation of harmful stereotypes. Stereotypes of Native Americans are male dominated and represent mainly Plains tribes—they fail to capture the diversity of Native people (and the 567 federally recognized tribes). They also create a culturally shallow picture for Native Americans to conform to—for instance, that all Native Americans wear feather headdresses. And when people inevitably do fail to conform to this stereotype, their credibility can be undermined ("You're not a real Native American").

SWITCH UP | *Is it possible to adopt the practices of another culture without causing harm? If a Francophile American makes French crêpes, is this appropriation, or something closer to appreciation?*
As bell hooks suggests, context is incredibly important here. The power dynamics between mainstream white culture and the minority and marginalized groups from whom they appropriate, are key to whether something should be classed as cultural appropriation.

FORGERIES & FAKES

THE MAIN CONCEPT | A forgery is an artifact—be it a painting, a sculpture, or a signature—that purports to be created by someone other than the actual creator, and was specifically made with the intention to deceive. One long-standing debate in the philosophy of art is over whether an artwork should be disvalued aesthetically if it is found to be a forgery. According to the "skeptical view," the forgery and the original are equal in aesthetic value if there are no observable differences between them. If we think, as many people do, that aesthetic value rests exclusively in appearance, it's hard to know what would ground the claim that one is, for instance, more beautiful than the other. However, as the American philosopher Nelson Goodman pointed out in *Languages of Art* (1968), irrespective of the accuracy of the "good" forgery, we do treat forgeries differently once they're exposed. Why is this? It may be because we place value on a piece of art being produced, authentically, by a particular "creative genius" with specific intentions and abilities. Our appreciation of artworks depends on them issuing from certain kinds of conscious, intentional processes. Forgeries disturb our stories about how good art is created.

DRILL DOWN | Is there really any salient difference between my copy of Amrita Sher-Gil's *Brahmacharis* and the original painting? Tomáš Kulka encourages us to distinguish between two types of value. On the one hand, there is art-historical value: Sher-Gil's original is value-worthy because it has a particular history, linking it to the painter (determinable through minute analysis of the painting materials). There is also, however, aesthetic value—where historical information may be utterly irrelevant. Two objects that are, to the eye, imperceptibly different can have a similar aesthetic value. Indeed, according to Kulka, a picture forged to look like it was painted by Sher-Gil might actually have higher aesthetic value, while having a lower art-historical one.

PRIVATE PROPERTY
Page 28

THE CATEGORY OF "ART"
Page 52

ORGANISMS & ARTIFACTS
Page 144

SWITCH UP | *One reason we may take issue with forgeries is because they seem in some way inauthentic. The notion of authenticity is of central importance to French existentialists like Simone de Beauvoir and Jean-Paul Sartre. Both foregrounded individual responsibility and self-determination in their work; as such, both may well have had concerns about forgeries, seeing them as inauthentic acts, and insincere expressions of the self.*

THE STANDARD OF TASTE

THE MAIN CONCEPT | At first glance, it seems clear that taste is subjective. You like mayonnaise and I hate it. Neither of us is right or wrong—it's just a matter of taste. At the same time, many of us think that some books, or movies, or meals, are obviously better or worse than others. Toni Morrison simply writes better novels than John Grisham. Fact. This is a puzzle that the eighteenth-century Scottish philosopher David Hume took as the subject of his essay "Of the Standard of Taste" (1752). Hume thought that agreement about aesthetic value pointed to decisive, objective standards, and his aim was to work out how to identify those standards. His solution was to look to "true judges"—people whose aesthetic senses are refined and well developed (for instance, wine connoisseurs)—and to look at the points where their verdicts about art overlapped. As he wrote, "a strong sense, united to delicate sentiment, improved by practice, perfected by comparison, and cleared of all prejudice, can alone entitle critics to this valuable character; and the joint verdict of such, wherever they are found, is the true standard of taste and beauty." Beauty, then, is apparently not just in the eye of the beholder—it can be objectively measured by a true judge.

DRILL DOWN | According to Hume, there are artworks "universally found to please in all countries in all ages." It's a dramatic claim without much evidential basis. Are all artworks, with their various linguistic and cultural peculiarities, equally accessible to all peoples? One critic of this account, Richard Shusterman, suggests Hume is insufficiently aware of the ways that aesthetic judgments are embedded in sociocultural contexts. Hume posits a supposedly "true" and "universal" measure of taste rather than seeing it as an "alterable product of social dynamics and history." And by positing true judges, Hume unfairly confers on certain people the right to say what is, or isn't, truly beautiful, while denying the same right to others.

BEAUTY
Page 54
A PRIORI KNOWLEDGE
Page 96
EPISTEMIC OPPRESSION
Page 100

SWITCH UP | *Can there be objective aesthetic truths? If your answer is "yes," you seem to be making a metaphysical claim: aesthetic judgments (about, say, whether or not something is beautiful) are true or false, irrespective of what humans believe. However, this view may run counter to certain intuitions. Consider, for instance, if it makes sense to say that you learned your favorite food wasn't, in fact, delicious?*

CULTURAL RELATIVISM

THE MAIN CONCEPT | According to Jewish and Christian traditions, Moses ascended Mount Sinai, where he was given ten statements of moral law, inscribed on stone by God. "Thou shalt honor thy father and mother," "Thou shalt not commit adultery," and so on. According to these traditions, the Ten Commandments are moral precepts for all human beings, everywhere. This, then, is an example of moral universalism—the thought that some things are right or wrong, for everyone, across all cultures. Universalism, however, is not unproblematic. For instance, some polyamorous societies are fully accepting of what other societies would consider adulterous relationships. So there is cross-cultural disagreement about such moral claims, just as there can be disagreement about table manners (in some cultures belching demonstrates appreciation of a meal; in others it's the height of rudeness). These considerations motivate a concern that claims about rightness or wrongness are culturally relative—they depend on the cultural context in which they're made. This may cause two types of worry. On the one hand, it may move us to question our certainty about what seem to be basic moral truths (is murder really wrong?). On the other, we may start to worry that opposing values block any kind of meaningful cross-cultural dialogue.

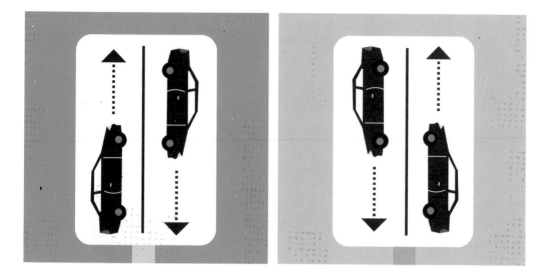

DRILL DOWN | Kwame Anthony Appiah is interested in differing cultural attitudes toward, among other things, sexuality. In one society, being gay may be uncontroversial—while in another it may be considered a sin. How can members of these different social groups hope to converse meaningfully when their views are so dramatically opposed? Appiah's point, found in his book *Cosmopolitanism* (2006), is not to get caught up brokering rational agreement. The discussion of normative issues is, in itself, a valuable exercise—not least, he says, because minds are often changed less through rational debate and settlement on a shared premise, than through exposure to, and familiarity with, alternative perspectives.

SWITCH UP | *When examining other social groups, the Indian feminist scholar Uma Narayan suggests that it's important to remember that one's own culture is far from perfect. Americans may be appalled at Indian "dowry murders" and take them as evidence of an unusually sexist society—but they should simultaneously recognize that there are similar (if not higher) rates of domestic violence and murder of women in the United States.*

QUEER THEORY
Page 40

MORAL REALISM
Page 42

EATING ANIMALS
Page 64

CENSORSHIP

THE MAIN CONCEPT | Government authorities exert a considerable amount of control over our cultural output. One form this control takes is censorship, the banning or suppression of materials, like books, movies, and music by the state (and only by the state). Often, censorship appears to be in direct conflict with what we call the "right to free speech." We should, we think, be allowed to express ourselves freely, in film or prose, without hindrance by the state or other people. This idea finds early form in John Stuart Mill's *On Liberty* (1859), coauthored with his wife, Harriet Taylor Mill. As one of the key architects of classical liberalism, Mill argued that individuals should be free from state intervention—except when their actions, or expressions, harm others. This is his "harm" or "liberty" principle. For Mill, if I freely express the opinion that "Bankers are scum" in the national press, nobody should intervene, although they may "remonstrate or entreat" me, using argument and discussion, to change my views. However, if I circulate pamphlets calling for bankers to be shot, state bodies like the police would be justified in intervening to stop me (by banning the material), because of the tangible risk of physical harm to others. This remains the stated reason behind much governmental censorship.

DRILL DOWN | There is considerable debate, inside and outside philosophy, over whether or not pornography should be censored. Mill's harm principle encourages us to reflect on what grounds there may be for state intervention. Feminist philosophers Rae Langton and Jennifer Hornsby follow the British and American courts in construing pornography as speech, and claim that, in representing women in subordinate and degrading positions, it constitutes "hate speech"—speech that harms others. On this view, pornography implies, and even presupposes, that women should be objectified—treated as objects rather than people. This may not have direct consequences for consenting sex-workers in pornographic movies, but it affects how women are seen and treated more widely in society.

SWITCH UP | *The American philosopher of language Jennifer Saul reminds us to be careful in our analysis of "speech acts." For something to count as speech rather than mere utterance, it needs to be read or heard unambiguously (rather than, for example, an ambiguous gargle). On Saul's account, pornography doesn't have a clear message. Viewing it as an utterance takes the force out of Langton and Hornsby's critique.*

THE SOCIAL CONTRACT
Page 18

INTERSECTIONALITY
Page 34

EPISTEMIC OPPRESSION
Page 100

"'It is certain, in any case, that ignorance, allied with power, is the most ferocious enemy justice can have."

JAMES BALDWIN,
NO NAME IN THE STREET (1972)

3

KNOWLEDGE

INTRODUCTION

Can you trust us? How do you know that we actually know what we're talking about? There's a chance (not a big one, admittedly, but a logical possibility) that we're a bunch of charlatans, making up stuff as we go along. Was there really a philosopher called Immanuel Kant? Can anyone seriously have thought that it's always wrong , in every single possible circumstance, to lie? Unless you already know enough philosophy to be able to fact-check, you're taking a risk trusting us.

Then again, maybe we know the history of Western philosophy inside out. But maybe we've decided to deceive you. Maybe we've smuggled in a few minor falsehoods here and there (have you checked all the dates?) Why? Just for the heck of it, perhaps. Given the whimsy of human nature it is, again, a possibility.

Or maybe we genuinely are three experts, working in different areas in academic philosophy, who've been commissioned by our publishers to write down what we know in as clear a way as possible. That's another possibility, isn't it? It's plausible that we genuinely want to share our knowledge with you—and maybe the fact that there are three of us actually makes us more reliable? We can cross-reference facts, troubleshoot difficult ideas, and pool our knowledge.

Enough about us. What about you? Can you trust yourself? Have there ever been times when you've read something (philosophical or otherwise) and it just hasn't gone in? You've tried and tried, but you just can't understand it. You think and think and think . . . and maybe eventually it seems to make a little bit of sense. But what if it doesn't? What if you've misunderstood it? How can you be sure that you know what you think you know?

What is knowledge?

All of these questions fall within the sphere of philosophy known as epistemology. This is the study of ("ology") knowledge ("episteme")—and in the Western tradition it's usually split into two areas. The first concerns the nature of knowledge. What is knowledge, exactly? The second concerns the limits of human knowledge. What things can we know? What things lie beyond the limits of human understanding?

In this chapter, we're going to be considering what knowledge is. Is it, as some epistemologists maintain, simply "justified true belief"? What's the difference between *a priori* and *a posteriori* knowledge? We'll be asking how we gain knowledge, how we produce it, and how people manipulate it. We're also going to be looking at ignorance—the state typically taken to be the obverse of knowledge. Following on from recent developments in (especially social) epistemology, we suggest some ways of problematizing our everyday understanding of this seemingly passive phenomenon.

We'll look at the ways that knowledge can be gleaned—whether through internal reasoning or via the scientific exercise of our senses—and extending the thoughts outlined above, we'll investigate the reach of the skeptical hypothesis: Who and what can you truly trust, and what makes our trust warranted? In examining these kinds of questions, we'll look at the way that thinkers like René Descartes used hyperbolic forms of skepticism in their philosophical projects.

The effects of knowledge

As part of all this, we're also going to be considering the effects of knowledge. Looking at W. E. B. Du Bois's notion of "double consciousness," and the work of social epistemologists like Kristie Dotson, we'll see how epistemic systems can do damage and oppress their willing (and unwilling) participants. Some kinds of knowledge are privileged over others, and these kinds of biases exist in all walks of life and all social settings—be it a school curriculum, or in a popular, introductory philosophy book.

The way this book has been written and structured, printed, and sold is the product of a particular kind of epistemic framework, a specific kind of knowledge production. Given this, we encourage you again to wonder: can you trust us? We hope so. We're trying to be reliable. Still, it's always worth checking.

TIMELINE

SYRIAN SOPHIST

In addition to being an empress, the Syrian sophist Julia Domna is a philosopher of renown, and her court in Rome frequently plays host to thinkers like Philostratus and Galen, and discussions on the nature of knowledge and its limits.

BIRTH OF MODERN PHILOSOPHY

This century sees the birth of Cartesian epistemology, with the popularization of discussions about skepticism and radical doubt. Rationalism in mainland Europe finds its partner in empiricist ideas in Britain (in the work of John Locke, Damaris Cudworth, and George Berkeley).

300 BCE **100 CE** **300** **1600**

FEMALE THINKERS

While Aristotle is expanding his elitist, men-only philosophy club, a group of Greek women are using principles introduced by Pythagorus to explore the nature of their own social realities. In works such as *On Wisdom* (c. 300 BCE), Perictione, Theano, and Aesara discuss moral psychology in relation to social standing.

CHRISTIANITY

Due to the influence of Emperor Constantine, Christianity becomes the dominant religion in the Mediterranean. Thinkers emerge to smooth the transition between the old philosophies and the new. Augustine, Bishop of Hippo, is one such scholar. His *Confessions* (c. 400 CE) uses Platonism to extrapolate Christian epistemology.

GENDER AND RACE

As part of the civil rights struggles in the US, Sojourner Truth and Anna Julia Cooper examine the epistemic positions inhabited by women of color in racist and sexist societies. W. E. B. Du Bois lays out his concept of "double consciousness" to describe the psychological damages done by oppressive societies.

NEW CHALLENGES

At the start of this new century, "fake news" and "post-truth" dominate public discourse, while decolonial student movements like "Why is my Curriculum White?" and #RhodesMustFall renew challenges to long-standing realities of whitewashing and erasure in schools, universities, and mainstream media.

| 1700 | 1800 | 1900 | 2000 |

DAVID HUME

Despite the muted response to his *Treatise* (1738), David Hume's work ultimately reinvigorates philosophical debates about the source of concepts, of knowledge, and the role of perception in these exchanges. Immanuel Kant cites Hume as the prompt for his various *Critiques*.

NEW PARADIGMS

Western epistemology shifts away from Cartesianism to other paradigms, especially social, feminist, and decolonial epistemologies. Classic contributions include Gayatri Spivak's "Can the Subaltern Speak?" and Patricia Hill Collins's *Black Feminist Thought* (1990).

BIOGRAPHIES

JOHN LOCKE (1632–1704)

Born to a Puritan family in Somerset, England, John Locke attended Oxford University, where he achieved a bachelor's degree in medicine. His work as a physician doubtless influenced his philosophical sensibilities (as is evident from his empiricist leanings), and simultaneously put him in contact with important political figures like the 1st Earl of Shaftesbury, Anthony Ashley Cooper. Locke worked in the sciences and for the government (on the Board of Trade and Plantations, which organized England's colonial affairs). This was undemanding work, apparently, since he also found time to write his mammoth *Essay Concerning Human Understanding* (1689). He met Damaris Cudworth in 1682, about whom we know much less. Largely self-educated—in the library of her father, the master of a Cambridge college—she was already familiar with Locke's work when they met. They enjoyed a mutually beneficial relationship that dwelled on issues of reason and faith, and the modes and manifestations of human knowledge. There was a romantic element to their connection, too, despite Cudworth's subsequent marriage to Sir Francis Masham. Locke never married, but lived with Damaris and her husband until his death.

DAVID HUME (1711–1776)

Born into a noble Scottish family, David Hume (originally Home) experienced a relatively impoverished childhood, brought up by his single mother, Katherine. Attending university aged 12, rather than the standard 14, he left before graduating, unimpressed by his teachers' abilities (or lack thereof). His first book, *A Treatise on Human Nature* (1738), was poorly received, but he achieved a certain amount of success—while a librarian at Edinburgh University—with his best-selling six-volume *History of England* (1754–61). His *Enquiry Concerning Human Understanding* (1748) and *An Enquiry Concerning the Principles of Morals* (1751) were the two books on which, at the end of his life, Hume wanted to be judged . . . but wasn't; his *Treatise* is standardly taken to be his richest work. Hume is known for his skepticism and his atheism, the latter costing him the oddly titled "Chair in Pneumatics and Moral Philosophy" at Edinburgh. It's notable that while his atheism was the subject of some censure, his contemporaries took less umbrage with the flagrantly racist views he expressed about "natural subordination" in his essay "Of National Characters."

W. E. B. DU BOIS (1868–1963)

William Edward Burghardt Du Bois grew up in Great Barrington, Massachusetts, where he attended a local integrated school. Following his academic successes, Du Bois decided to apply to college and—supported by donations from his church—achieved a place at Fisk University in Tennessee. There, he witnessed the profound effects of Southern racism in the form of lynchings and the Jim Crow laws—experiences that shaped his future research. Largely self-funded, Du Bois went to Harvard (where he was taught by the philosopher William James), and in 1895 he was the first African American to be awarded a PhD from that university. His work spanned sociology, activism, and philosophy. *The Philadelphia Negro* (1899) was borne out of his field research into African-American social issues in that city (and is one of the first cases of a statistically grounded sociological study). His best-known text is *The Souls of Black Folk* (1903), in which he put forward his notion of "double consciousness." A critic of capitalism and advocate of Marxism, Du Bois came under government scrutiny in the 1950s. He was tried in 1951 and though the case was dismissed, his passport was confiscated for the next eight years.

KRISTIE DOTSON (1975–)

Born into a working-class, single-parent family in the United States, black philosopher Kristie Dotson says her keen awareness of the myriad ways that society silences people began when she experienced homelessness as a teenager. Through repeated attempts to communicate her family's circumstances, Dotson realized that "incapacitating silencing" exacerbated the oppression of already-suffering people. These early experiences shaped her future work on epistemic oppression—an "inheritance" of 200 years of black feminist social theory, inspired by thinkers like Audre Lorde, Hortense Spillers, and Patricia Hill Collins. One of her most significant contributions to philosophy includes her metaphilosophy. For example, in "Between Rocks and Hard Places" (2016) she develops an account of black feminist professional philosophy that challenges whether originality or fundamentality are desirable, or even possible, guiding principles for philosophical work. Dotson's theoretical work informs her political activism and vice versa. She works on various projects aimed at improving social, political, and economic outcomes for cis- and transgender black women and girls.

WHAT IS KNOWLEDGE?

THE MAIN CONCEPT | What do we mean when we say that we know something? One long-standing definition is that knowledge is a particular kind of mental state, like a want, hope, or desire. More specifically, it's a kind of belief—a justified, true belief ("JTB"). Let's break this down. The so-called JTB account is a propositional account of knowledge; it's focused on propositions—statements like "I believe that the Earth is flat," "I believe that the square root of 64 is 8," or "I believe that it is 2pm." Some of these beliefs are true (the square root of 64 is 8) and some of them are false (the Earth isn't flat). Some of these beliefs are justified as well, because they're supported by good evidence or reasoning. Your belief that it is 2pm might be true (it is, actually, 2pm), and this belief may be justified, based as it is on the evidence supplied to you by your analog wristwatch. It may also be true and unjustified—if your wristwatch, unbeknownst to you, broke 24 hours earlier, at 2pm. According to JTB, to have knowledge you must have a belief that something is the case, it must be true that this something actually is the case, and your true belief needs to be justified.

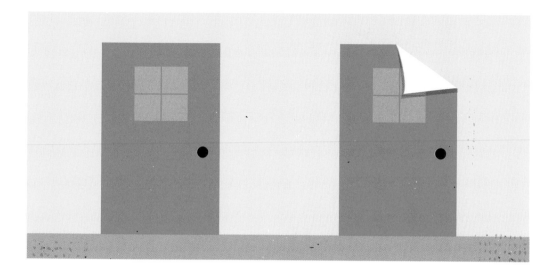

DRILL DOWN | Imagine you're driving through the countryside. From afar, you spy something that looks exactly like a barn—so you believe you're seeing a barn. And you are! Without realizing, however, you happen to be driving through a neighborhood where there are a bunch of fake barns—mere facades. If you'd been looking at one of the fake barns you'd have believed (falsely) that you were seeing a barn. Your belief is true and justified, but it's only luck that you were looking at a real barn. This thought experiment, developed by US philosopher Alvin Goldman, is an example of a "Gettier case"—named after Edmund Gettier, who used similar examples to challenge the JTB account of knowledge.

SWITCH UP | *In "The Inescapability of Gettier Problems" (1994), Linda Zagzebski identifies a notable lack of progress in discussions about knowledge and Gettier cases. This may be because Gettier puzzles are intractable; there is, Zagzebski suggests, no possible extra condition that could make JTB resistant to counterexamples. And the very method of discussion itself may also be flawed—intuitions about stories may not be the best way to achieve knowledge about knowledge.*

SKEPTICISM

THE MAIN CONCEPT | Philosophers have always been doubtful about our ability to know things. These things could include mathematical propositions, or the truth of God's existence, or facts about the external world. Gorgias and Cratylus were two sophists (itinerant teachers) who believed that there are any number of reasons for us to be suspicious of our own and other people's claims to knowledge—if there's one thing we can be relatively sure of, it's that human beings are fallible creatures. We make errors when we're reasoning. It's easy, for instance, to mess up long division. We can be misled by the testimony of others. We also know that our senses are prey to illusions—is that bucket of water extremely hot or extremely cold? Is that distant tower cuboid or cylindrical? René Descartes focused on dreams as a source of doubt. Can you, for example, be certain that you're not dreaming right now? He went further still and asked how we could be sure that we're not subject to the machinations of a powerful demon, making us think we're experiencing things that we're not (like the movie *The Matrix* . . . but in seventeenth-century France). These are all reasons, the skeptic says, to lose confidence in what we think we know.

DRILL DOWN | Skepticism is sometimes used as a rhetorical position. Descartes wasn't a genuine skeptic—rather, he presented a picture of radical doubt in order to showcase his response to it. His response finds succinct form in the *Cogito* argument: *Cogito, ergo sum* ("I think, therefore I am"). A demon might confuse you into thinking you're experiencing something you're not, but as soon as you start considering this possibility—that you're subject to illusion—you perform a mental process (doubting). Doing this, you can be sure of at least one thing: that you, the thinking, doubting being, actually exist! Descartes used this as the "Archimedean point" (a sturdy point from which one can get purchase on an issue) around which he developed his system of knowledge.

PERCEPTION
Page 92
SUBSTANCE DUALISM
Page 124
PHENOMENOLOGY
Page 126

SWITCH UP | *Philosophers from Søren Kierkegaard to Friedrich Nietzsche have been skeptical about the success of Descartes's* Cogito. *Can we really say there's a discrete "I" doing the thinking? Ghanaian theologian J. S. Pobee says the argument is characteristic of the Western focus on the individual, and he suggests an alternative formulation grounded in the community-focused Hunhu/Ubuntu tradition:* Cognatus, ergo sum. *I belong to a family, therefore I exist.*

IGNORANCE

THE MAIN CONCEPT | Traditionally, ignorance is understood as a lack or absence of knowledge. We're ignorant of things we happen not to know because we haven't learned them yet (I am ignorant of central truths in farming), or because it's not yet possible to know them (Will it rain in Vancouver in June 2091?). Ignorance can play an important role in producing knowledge. One hallmark of good science is the "double-blind randomized trial," where generating reliable results depends on researchers and participants *not* knowing whether the drug they are testing is genuine or a placebo. But ignorance can also get in the way of knowledge, as well as being something that is actively produced. Nancy Tuana identifies various forms of "active ignorance" in, for example, women's medicine. "Knowing that we don't know, but not caring to know" has undermined research into a contraceptive pill for men. Sometimes, we don't even know that we don't know, because our current interests and knowledge—or what we think of as knowledge—blocks further scientific inquiry into topics like the structure of the clitoris or women's cardiac illness. Similarly, certain types of knowledge are sometimes deemed too inconvenient to be shared widely or with certain populations, such as keeping information about the health risks associated with smoking from the general public, with some tobacco companies even claiming that "doubt is our product."

DRILL DOWN | Charles W. Mills, inspired by standpoint theory (see page 104) and the work of thinkers like W. E. B. Du Bois, argues that whole political systems—as well as the individuals that populate them—can produce ignorance. In societies with significant histories of racism, the social and political system relies on epistemological mechanisms that encourage the erasure and denial of important truths about racism and its origins, as well as discrediting the intellectual, social, and political labor of people of color. He calls this an "epistemology of ignorance." This ignorance is not just active, but "resistant." Even with considerable evidence available, it can seem almost impossible to dislodge the long-standing, durable mythologies that such ignorance produces.

SWITCH UP | *While public discussion focuses on fake news and post-truth, American epistemologists Rachel V. McKinnon and Jason Stanley have demonstrated that actively produced ignorance—in the form of propaganda— is nothing new, even if new media provide new methods for generating it. McKinnon and Stanley suggest different ways for us to combat misinformation, and emphasize the importance of studying historical manifestations of ignorance in this process.*

WHITE SUPREMACY
Page 30
SOCIAL EPISTEMOLOGY
Page 98
STANDPOINT THEORY
Page 104

PERCEPTION

THE MAIN CONCEPT | Our senses—sight, hearing, touch, taste, and smell—appear to give us access to the world around us. We can smell flowers, taste strawberries, see sunsets, and so on. But do we perceive the world directly? The thesis that we do is called "direct realism," or "naive realism." The naive realist says that when I smell a rose, I directly perceive a real property of that real rose. But are things actually so straightforward? Our perception of objects often changes without any corresponding changes in the objects themselves. The hum from a computer will sound louder the closer you are to it. Seen from one angle, a plate may appear round—from another, ovoid. We know these perceptual variations aren't variations in the objects themselves (plates don't mutate)—and this leads to the curious conclusion that the way I perceive such things might not correlate to how these things actually are. Perhaps the mutating plate is a mental object, or "sense datum," as Bertrand Russell termed it. This "argument from perceptual variation" leads to the thought that we don't, in fact, perceive the world directly. Collections of ideas (sense data, see opposite) stand as intermediaries through which we gain indirect access to the real world (hence "indirect realism").

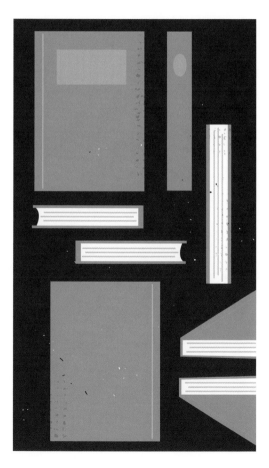

DRILL DOWN | Can we have direct knowledge of the external world? The eighteenth-century Irish philosopher Bishop George Berkeley gave a rather extreme answer to this question. He declared, "There are no material things"; the physical objects that we perceive around us are nothing more than collections of ideas ("sense data"). As such, he said, all worldly objects are dependent on perceiving minds for their existence. "To be is to be perceived." The peculiar upshot of Berkeley's idealism (the view that reality is made up of nothing more than ideas and the minds that perceive them) is that when we do not perceive the objects in the world . . . they simply don't exist.

SWITCH UP | *British idealism was highly fashionable at the start of the twentieth century. F. H. Bradley and J. M. E. McTaggart both endorsed it, inspired by Berkeley—but it was more profoundly influenced by G. W. F. Hegel and Johann Gottlieb Fichte. This connection to German philosophy may also have led to the downfall of British idealism, when Bertrand Russell began to associate Hegel and Fichte with other forms of German thought— specifically those found in Nazi ideology.*

EMPIRICISM

THE MAIN CONCEPT | Empirical knowledge is knowledge acquired through the senses. Empiricism is the thesis that all human knowledge either is, or is dependent on, empirical knowledge. This position is captured by the Latin slogan, *Nihil est in intellectu quod non sit prius in sensu* ("Nothing is in the intellect that was not first in the senses"). In the history of Western philosophy, John Locke and David Hume are among the most well-known empiricists. Both endorsed some form of the above, and rejected the idea that we might have any kind of innate knowledge (knowledge that we're born with). Empiricists believe that we're born blank, a *tabula rasa* (blank or clean slate) on which experience then draws. The innatist view, on the other hand, is associated with the rationalist tradition exemplified by philosophers like Gottfried Wilhelm Leibniz, who believed that there are some ideas that we have baked into our brains. According to both Leibniz and Descartes, for example, mathematical truths are evident to us without empirical evidence; they may not always be immediately obvious, but they are a structural part of our thinking, and can be coaxed out with the right questions. The rationalist position is seen to be supported by the "argument from universal assent" (that there are some facts—for example, about mathematics— that everyone agrees upon).

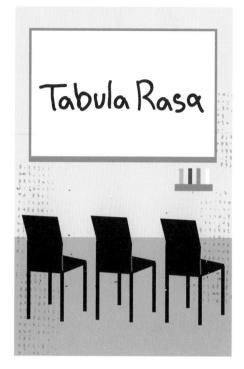

DRILL DOWN | Traditionally, empiricists are differentiated from rationalists in relation to their views on the "intuition/deduction" thesis. This holds that some things are knowable to us only via intuition, and that other things can be deduced from these intuited facts. Intuition in this context is the ability to understand something as true without explicit reasoning; for example, it's obvious that 4 is greater than 3. Deduction is the process by which one thing can be worked out on the basis of some other thing, using logic alone. For instance, we can deduce from the above that there is at least one number greater than 3. Empiricists are suspicious of the idea that one can clearly and distinctly intuit some truth without reasoning.

SWITCH UP | *In the standard story, Descartes and Leibniz are Continental rationalists, while Locke, Berkeley, and Hume are British empiricists. Historians of ideas, however, have criticized the empiricist/rationalist distinction for being too simplistic. Whether or not you're an empiricist will depend on the domain of knowledge you're working within (you might be able to intuit mathematical truths, but not ethical ones, for example). Philosopher of early modernism Chris Meyns suggests the line could be better drawn between "speculative" and "experimental" philosophers.*

A PRIORI KNOWLEDGE

THE MAIN CONCEPT | We come to learn things in different ways. Sometimes, we learn things after having experienced them—for example, that fire is hot, and sugar is sweet. Then there's knowledge we can have even before we've consulted the senses. There are, seemingly, propositions we come to understand through the use of reason alone. Take mathematical knowledge. To find out the truth of "2 + 2 = 4," you don't have to look at anything in the world. You can just think about it. The same is true for a statement like "All crows are birds." If you understand the concepts "crow" and "bird," you know that the statement tracks the truth. Knowledge that we gain prior to sense experience and the analysis of empirical facts is called (for obvious reasons) *a priori* knowledge. It's contrasted with *a posteriori* knowledge— knowledge that comes after, or posterior to, consultation of the senses; for instance, in order to learn whether it's raining outside, you have to check the world, rather than simply contemplate the question. Propositions can be either *a priori* or *a posteriori*—and the same is true for arguments. An *a posteriori* argument is one where at least one of the premises is an *a posteriori* proposition. The premises of an *a priori* argument are supposedly all evident from reason alone.

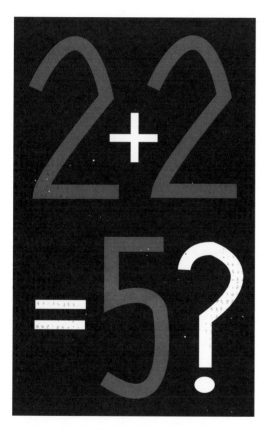

DRILL DOWN | The *a priori/ a posteriori* distinction is often confused with the "analytic/synthetic" distinction. A statement like "All crows are birds" is analytic because the concept "bird" is nested within the concept "crow." Through conceptual analysis you can unpack the former out of the latter. A statement like "Pittsburgh is located 8,000 miles from Mumbai" is synthetic because the idea of being located a specific distance from Mumbai is not contained within the concept of Pittsburgh. It's an additional idea—and the statement is a synthesis of the first concept and some further facts. Typically, these further facts are empirical, which is why synthetic statements often overlap *a posteriori* ones.

SWITCH UP | A prioricity *and a posteriocity can also be confused with necessity and contingency. A necessary fact is one that is always true in every possible world. A contingent fact is one that depends upon—is contingent on—this world, but not all possible worlds. A priori knowledge appears to be necessary—but are all necessary propositions a priori?*

SOCIAL EPISTEMOLOGY

THE MAIN CONCEPT | Historically, philosophers interested in questions about knowledge (epistemologists) have focused on how particular individuals came to acquire, and justify, their beliefs. This way of thinking imagines that most philosophically interesting cases of knowledge or belief arise through individual knowers observing the world, or their own experience, and reflecting on the evidence using their own powers of reasoning. In the twentieth century, philosophers like Lorraine Code challenged this model, arguing that knowing is an importantly—and perhaps, essentially—social phenomenon. So much of our knowledge seems to rely on other people, especially their verbal or written testimony: teachers, authors, scientists, kind strangers who give us directions when we are lost. Even for individuals, knowing seems to be an interpersonal phenomenon. Knowing can be social in other ways, too. American epistemologist Alvin Goldman notes that we ascribe knowledge to collectives—like juries, governments, or football teams—who make judgments about what beliefs are true or justified as groups. Humans have also invented social systems designed to convincingly produce and evaluate knowledge. The processes involved in verifying and replicating scientific findings are just one example (see page 102).

DRILL DOWN | One of the most important ways that individuals come to acquire knowledge socially occurs through testimony—the intentional transfer of a belief from one person to another. This often happens through speech, but it can also happen through writing, or other forms of signaling (art, dance, even semaphore). Acquiring knowledge through testimony requires trusting that those from whom we receive it are honest, and not in error. This puts hearers in a vulnerable position. What reason is there, if any, to trust that speakers aren't deceiving us, or just plain wrong? Why should we ascribe "epistemic authority" to speakers and their testimony? What are the consequences if we don't?

SKEPTICISM
Page 88

EPISTEMIC OPPRESSION
Page 100

STANDPOINT THEORY
Page 104

SWITCH UP | *If knowing is social, then a person's social situation and relationship to other knowers seems to matter a great deal to what and how they can know. Feminist epistemologists, including those concerned with epistemic oppression and standpoint theory (see pages 100 and 104), have emphasized that knowers are "socially situated." Knowers are not disembodied minds processing information, but embodied subjects with different experiences and perspectives.*

EPISTEMIC OPPRESSION

THE MAIN CONCEPT | The American philosopher Kristie Dotson argues that, as well as social and political forms of oppression, epistemic oppression exists, too. Societies rely on what she calls "shared epistemic resources": common understandings of what is "known" (facts about science, human bodies, or social phenomena); what criteria claims must meet to count as "knowledge"; and which people are "knowers" (experts or teachers). But not all groups enjoy equal opportunities when it comes to using these resources. This hampers their ability to communicate their claims effectively to audiences who themselves lack, ignore, or refuse the epistemic resources needed to make sense of those claims. They may also lack access to intellectual traditions that make sense of their experiences, and they may struggle in the absence of fair and accurate standards by which their claims to knowledge will be judged as truthful or knowledgeable. Following sociologist Patricia Hill Collins, Dotson has developed this idea by highlighting how, despite a centuries-long history, black feminist thought on knowledge and ignorance has been suppressed, omitted from mainstream scholarship, and trivialized. Black women are epistemically oppressed since dominant shared epistemic resources fail to conceptualize their experiences or recognize their truth claims as knowledge.

DRILL DOWN | British epistemologist Miranda Fricker offers us a similar concept: epistemic injustice. Here, someone is wronged not just as a person, but as someone capable of creating, detecting, and sharing knowledge. This is because of how social power affects our practices around knowledge. In Patricia Highsmith's novel *The Talented Mr Ripley* (1955), a woman's attempts to report the facts about her partner's disappearance are dismissed because she is considered emotional and unreliable. Negative stereotypes about women prejudice her audience against her efforts to communicate knowledge. Similarly, Fricker argues that people can struggle to make sense of their experiences because they lack the concepts needed to do so. Before the concept of "sexual harassment" existed, those subjected to unwanted sexual attention at work struggled to make sense of—and make knowledge claims about—their experiences.

INTERSECTIONALITY
Page 34
DISABILITY
Page 36
IGNORANCE
Page 90
STANDPOINT THEORY
Page 104

SWITCH UP | *Sometimes those who don't experience a form of oppression expect to be educated about it by those burdened by its experiences, rather than proactively educating themselves. Worse, when educational labor is offered, it can be met by resilient skepticism or ignorance. According to American philosopher Nora Berenstain, such exchanges can constitute "epistemic exploitation."*

SCIENTIFIC KNOWLEDGE

THE MAIN CONCEPT | Science is one of humanity's most successful ways of producing knowledge. People have always sought to understand how human reasoning might combine with our powers of observation to generate knowledge that was thought to be more certain, and less prone to error. Science relies on a scientific method, where scientists collect and measure observable data to produce hypotheses that can be used to generate descriptions, explanations, and predictions about the world, which can then be tested by other scientists for accuracy, reliability, and replicability. Scientists rely on a combination of deductive, inductive, and abductive reasoning, as well as the creation of models, thought experiments, and computer simulations, to draw conclusions and to justify their knowledge claims. Twentieth-century philosophers of science Karl Popper and Thomas Kuhn revolutionized the philosophy of science in different ways. For Popper, science progressed through systematic attempts to falsify hypotheses using deductive methods. For Kuhn, the historical context and cultures of working scientists played as much of a role in generating scientific knowledge as any supposedly "universal" scientific method, generating "paradigms" that would only "shift" when those who subscribed to them retired or died.

DRILL DOWN | An old but famous problem for scientific knowledge was posed by David Hume. His "problem of induction" argued that no matter how much evidence we collect, the conclusion of an inductive argument is never guaranteed. For example, suppose that you infer, based on all the swans you have ever seen—and you've seen hundreds of swans—that it's true that "All swans are white." Your observations seem to justify this general conclusion. But as it turns out, it's false that all swans are white: black swans exist in Australasia. Drawing conclusions based on past observations offers no certainty that future observations will resemble them. If this is true, then just how authoritative is scientific knowledge?

SWITCH UP | *The feminist philosopher of science Evelyn Fox Keller has drawn attention to the gendered language of scientific discourse. Despite claims to linguistic neutrality, scientists often use problematic metaphors—like sixteenth-century English philosopher, Francis Bacon's troubling construal of nature: "I am come in very truth leading to you Nature with all her children to bind her to your service and make her your slave."*

STANDPOINT THEORY

THE MAIN CONCEPT | The growth of feminist movements in the second half of the twentieth century revealed that widely accepted examples of knowledge were actually based on problematic assumptions about gender. Standpoint theory, developed by feminist epistemologists like Sandra Harding and Nancy Hartsock, explained this by drawing on Marx's idea that socially disadvantaged groups—like women and the working class—are better able to perceive certain features of social reality; the experience of discrimination and disadvantage can provide an "epistemic advantage." Women's standpoint, for example, tracks the domestic, emotional, and child-rearing labor typically cast as "women's work," and not the sort of work that contributes to society. Even among women, class and race differences will generate different standpoints: while some women know only the drudgery of housework, others will also have to contend with poorly paid work as the household breadwinner. The feminist philosopher Alison Jaggar notes that, rather than being automatically available, a standpoint is "achieved": a way of thinking about reality that reflects a marginalized group's interests and understands their own interpretations of their experiences as knowledge.

DRILL DOWN | The Indian feminist scholar Uma Narayan argues that, from the perspective of women living in colonized countries, the "double vision" offered by achieving a feminist standpoint can be complicated and troublesome. The social costs of rejecting dominant, Western modes of knowing can result in the loss of access to power structures in society, while colonization often results in the erasure of knowledge of one's own culture. This can undermine one's ability to think or know from both social positions. The postmodern theorist Susan Hekman contends that standpoint theory's claim to better grasp reality fails to acknowledge that all perspectives are constituted through ways of talking and thinking that are themselves partial and dependent on context.

SWITCH UP | *One consequence of emphasizing the social context of knowledge is that these epistemologists offer a fundamental challenge to ideas about objectivity and the possibility of an impartial, disembodied perspective. Donna Haraway calls for a feminist objectivity that, in embracing "situated knowledge," denies that objectivity can be found in quests to transcend our bodies, or efforts to split knowers from what knowledge is about.*

THE MEDICAL GAZE

THE MAIN CONCEPT | In most societies, doctors are highly respected authorities in the domain of medical knowledge. They ask patients questions like, "Where does it hurt?" or "Is this painful?" They'll use stethoscopes and other equipment to gain information about your ailment, usually by trying to find where the problem is—in what body part or organ. French philosopher Michel Foucault argued in *The Birth of the Clinic* (1963) that this has not always been the primary diagnostic tactic of the physician. Questions that focus on individual organs and the site of disease, result from a particular, historically contingent framework that he called "the medical gaze." Before the advent of modern medicine, physicians were more likely to ask, "What's the matter with you?" They would build a diagnosis based on the patient's own perception of their ailment. For Foucault, political factors in eighteenth-century French society, from epidemics to the French Revolution, inaugurated a shift in attitudes. Rather than seeing a patient as a whole person, physicians began to view them as a set of functional or dysfunctional organs. Foucault argued that, while modern medicine has provided us with more effective drugs and treatments, this construction of medical knowledge results in a troubling and dehumanizing "dissection" of patients into their constituent parts.

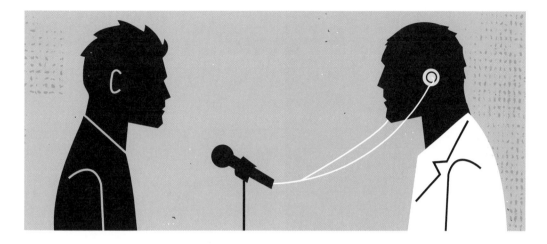

DRILL DOWN | Medical knowledge is most commonly associated with managing individual bodies. Foucault offers another insight: it can also be used to manage populations. In *The History of Sexuality* (1978), he introduced the notion of "biopower." Medical knowledge is deployed by the state to organize people and their lives: registering births and deaths to track the size of populations, monitoring populations for illness—especially hereditary disease—as well as productivity, and managing those who fail to conform to "normal" expectations by using medical institutions like hospitals and sanitoriums. This idea breaks from previous knowledge about power. Rather than something that can be possessed, surrendered, or traded by subjects, power makes up subjects, who exercise it in different ways.

SWITCH UP | *In a more recent shift in medical knowledge, the intimate, everyday knowledge possessed by patients with chronic illness has led to the recognition of "patient experts." But since most patients lack technical medical knowledge or training, how should we understand such knowledge? Philosopher Andrew Edgar contends that expert patient knowledge might helpfully be understood as a form of knowing through storytelling, or narrative construction.*

THE SOCIAL CONTRACT
Page 18
DISABILITY
Page 36
BIOLOGICAL CREATION
Page 132

DOUBLE CONSCIOUSNESS

THE MAIN CONCEPT | The term "double consciousness" was coined and developed by W. E. B. Du Bois. Introduced in *The Souls of Black Folk* (1903), it describes a particular epistemological position inhabited by African Americans, in which the unity of one's identity and selfhood is threatened by social oppression. Du Bois writes, "It is a peculiar sensation, this double-consciousness, this sense of always looking at one's self through the eyes of others, of measuring one's soul by the tape of a world that looks on in amused contempt and pity." In racist societies, such as the one in which Du Bois was writing, there are oppressive social scripts that describe black Americans in a dehumanizing way. This narrative clashes with the black American's own sense of identity—as a human—and the result is a fractured self. Society tells you you're one thing, while your own experience of yourself says you're another. As Du Bois powerfully puts it: "[o]ne feels his two-ness, an American, a Negro; two souls; two thoughts, two unreconciled strivings; two warring ideals in one dark body, whose dogged strength alone keeps it from being torn asunder." The concept of double consciousness has had considerable influence, shaping the work of writers and thinkers from Ralph Ellison and Toni Morrison to Jordan Peele.

WHITE SUPREMACY
Page 30

EPISTEMIC OPPRESSION
Page 100

STANDPOINT THEORY
Page 104

PHENOMENOLOGY
Page 126

DRILL DOWN | In *Darkwater: Voices from Within the Veil* (1920), Du Bois extended his concept of double consciousness to develop the notion of "second sight." People whose sense of self is fractured by social oppression have privileged epistemic insight. Unlike white Americans, who possess only "single sight" (being immersed in, and not victims of, the dominant and oppressive status quo), black Americans understand the reality of racism and oppression. This theoretical framework shares much with that of Anna Julia Cooper—as described in *A Voice from the South by a Black Woman of the South* (1892)—and paved the way, in part, for Sandra Harding's standpoint theory (see page 104).

SWITCH UP | *In 1949, Du Bois traveled to Warsaw and observed the destruction of the city and the Jewish Ghetto. Some commentators have suggested that his essay about this experience, "The Negro and the Warsaw Ghetto," implies a broadening of the concept of double consciousness to encapsulate the experience of other marginalized groups. Does this risk damaging the original concept?*

MEMORY

THE MAIN CONCEPT | The precise nature of memory has been the subject of contention for thousands of years—for as long as anyone can remember. According to some, memory is simply a static repository of information; in Augustine's fourth-century *Confessions* (397 CE), for example, memory is a storehouse, in which perception logs images for later retrieval, with some things becoming harder to access, the more you pile in. This storehouse view has been challenged by contemporary philosophers and psychologists, who have shown that memory is far from a passive vessel, but rather a capacity that expands and shapes information according to context. Recollection isn't just a matter of information retrieval, it's about generating specific representations of the past. And of course, talking about memory as if it's some single, determinate process is misleading, too. From Plato to Henri Bergson, and to more recent thinkers such as Lisa Baraitser, philosophers have recognized there are different kinds of memory, puzzling over the contrast between memories and sense perception. When you remember an experience, how does that mental state differ from the original phenomenological event? To invoke the famous example from French author Marcel Proust's *In Search of Lost Time* (1908), what is the difference between the taste of a madeleine and the memory of that taste?

DRILL DOWN | Just as there are different types of remembering, there are also different types of forgetting. You can forget how to bake, for instance, and you can forget facts—like the name of your friend's cat. Sometimes, you remember facts but forget how you came to know them; you remember your friend's cat is called Suzie but can't remember how you came to know this. The forgetting of "original evidence" is important in discussions around "evidentialism." Evidentialists hold that you're justified in having an attitude toward something (believing this cat is called Suzie) because you have good evidence for that thing. If you forget the evidence for your belief, as we often do, that seems to render your belief unjustified.

SWITCH UP | *Does a memory have to be accurate to be true? In her analysis of trauma, scholar Kelly Oliver gives the example of a Holocaust survivor recounting uprisings at Auschwitz. While historians say that only one of the camp's chimneys was set alight, the survivor stated that four were burned. Oliver suggests that this testimony captures an otherwise inexpressible truth that lies beyond the merely factual.*

"Rather than worrying, *what is gender, really?* or *what is race, really?* I think we should begin by asking what, if anything, we want them to be."

SALLY HASLANGER
"GENDER AND RACE" (2000)

4

REALITY

INTRODUCTION

Reality. It's pretty hard to get your head around. It includes absolutely everything. It includes all the existing things (the birds, the bees, the atoms, the solar systems) and—depending on your philosophical inclinations—all the nonexisting things as well (the unicorns, fictional characters, and so on). Philosophers, who are not known for their intellectual modesty, have been largely undaunted by its infinite breadth and profundity. Time and again throughout the history of Western philosophy they have taken reality—what is, and how it is—as their subject.

Metaphysics

In mainstream Euro-American thought, the study of reality has come to be called "metaphysics"—a term that is itself the focus of some controversy. Like other "meta"-words ("meta-language" or "meta-ethics"), metaphysics gives the impression of a science that goes beyond something else. Physics deals with matter, its behaviors and motions, the ins and outs of protons, neutrons, and quarks. Metaphysics, on the above understanding, goes beyond all that. It's not interested in gravity or mechanical laws of motion, but in a much more abstract, meta-level analysis.

A more mundane explanation holds that "metaphysics" derives from the work that Aristotle produced (including books on theology, wisdom, and the good life) after his *Physics*. Here, meta-physics, or "after the physics" is simply the product of an editorial decision—by Andronicus of Rhodes.

Whatever the etymology, the subject is now taken to encapsulate abstract questions about space, time, identity, and existence. Metaphysicians study what it is for things to exist, what it is to be real, and how reality is structured. They're not just interested in atoms or quarks; they're interested in the bigger stuff too, like humans, trees, and planets. Nor are their investigations restricted to material objects. Metaphysicians are fascinated by immaterial entities like angels, gods, and (less controversially) numbers. Are the numbers 3 and 4 real? Such things appear to abide by specific laws, independent of human concerns—which is why we discover, rather than create, mathematical truths)—but if asked to point to where the number 0 was discovered, you'd be stumped.

Different realities

This chapter examines reality from a number of angles. As well as looking at the metaphysical makeup of everyday objects, there are sections on the nature of time, the way we partition the world into apparently "natural kinds," and the existence of God. The intersection of religion and philosophy is a subject for a much bigger book, but in this chapter—as in the others—philosophical thought is heavily influenced by thinkers from a variety of faiths.

We also have discussions of dualism (the view that reality is constituted by mental and physical substances) and phenomenology (which studies the reality of experiential awareness). From Aristotle onward, metaphysics has intersected with interests in the biological realm, and we have tried to honor the strong conceptual connections between these two disciplines with entries on biological creation and biological essentialism.

Is reality trending yet?

Like all established systems of knowledge, Western metaphysics exhibits trends. Accounts of how things really are come in and go out of fashion. In the mid-nineteenth century, metaphysicians thought the structure and appearance of the world depended on human minds and ideas. In the twentieth century, the logical empiricists shunned metaphysical projects as unscientific and meaningless. These views were, in turn, transmuted into the scientistic musings that dominated the 1950s and 1960s. For a time, Western metaphysics became a matter of counting—which things exist, which don't; of crossing things off on an ontological call-sheet.

Trends and countertrends in metaphysics will doubtless continue. This year, reality may be a single indivisible whole. Next year, it may be nothing more than a mass of particles or gunk. One thought threaded throughout the following entries (and focused on in the entry on social ontology) is that these varying accounts of reality should be taken with a pinch of salt. When a metaphysician tells you how the world really, truly is, it's worth asking whether they benefit from seeing reality in that way. Chances are they do.

TIMELINE

NORMAN CONQUEST
The Norman-French army is victorious at the Battle of Hastings. Thus starts William of Normandy's rule and an influx of philosophical thought from France to Britain. The French cleric Anselm arrives in Canterbury, where he writes his *Proslogion*, aiming to prove God's existence.

ENLIGHTENMENT
The Age of Enlightenment sees a rejection of Aristotelian scholasticism. In conversation with Marin Mersenne and Elisabeth of Bohemia, René Descartes develops his influential dualistic metaphysics, which posits the existence of two distinct metaphysical substances: mind and body.

 **300 BCE** **1066 CE** 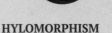 **1200** **1600**

ARISTOTLE
Aristotle's student—Alexander the Great—invades swathes of Asia and Africa. Aristotle, meanwhile, founds his Lyceum, where the work of the "philosopher" encapsulates activities as diverse as physics, politics, and medicine. What we now know as metaphysics was seen to be intimately connected to all these different areas.

HYLOMORPHISM
Following in the footsteps of Ibn Rushd (Averroes), the medieval scholastics Thomas Aquinas and Duns Scotus begin to interpret Christian doctrine in the light of Aristotle's metaphysics. Aristotle's proposal that beings are a compound of matter and form (hylomorphism) becomes *de rigueur* in Europe, enforced by the Catholic Church.

IDEALISM AND MORE

Influenced by the work of G. W. F. Hegel, R. G. Collingwood and F. H. Bradley develop a form of British idealism. The mind, they believe, has some part to play in the creation of reality. In Denmark, Søren Kierkegaard trials a form of existentialism, and in Middlesex, England, Mary Everest Boole compares Greek and Hindu logics.

A POLITICAL PROGRAM

While some schools of Euro-American metaphysics continue to focus on traditional issues, an increasing number of philosophers—from Judith Butler to Sally Haslanger and Arianne Shahvisi—are investigating the ways that the standard puzzles and questions intersect with pressing sociopolitical concerns. Metaphysics is not an objective philosophical practice: it's a political program.

1700 — **1800** — **1900** — **2000**

THE BIRTH OF MODERN SCIENCE

Advances in modern scientific method see the creation of new disciplinary boundaries. Where previously "natural philosophers" had studied what we would now call "science," metaphysical inquiry begins to become less obviously necessary for scientific inquiry. Philosophers become distinct from scientists.

POSTWAR THEORIES

By mid-century, British idealism is on the way out, partly because of its perceived associations with the German intellectual tradition (and World War II). Phenomenology is on the up in France. And logical positivism, developed in Austria, begins to appear in the UK and US as philosophers flee war-torn Europe.

BIOGRAPHIES

ARISTOTLE (384–322 BCE)

Aristotle was orphaned when young and raised in the Macedonian court where his father had been a physician. He was encouraged to attend Plato's elite Academy, remaining a member for many years; he studied under Plato (who had studied under Socrates), and went on to tutor Alexander the Great, before founding his own school, the Lyceum. Our modern understanding of philosophy doesn't really cover the extent of Aristotle's interests—he dabbled in everything, from astrology to zoology. In the *Metaphysics*, he argued for hylomorphism—that things are made up of both matter and form—as opposed to Plato's view that reality is dependent on "Forms" (see page 42). In *De Anima*, Aristotle expressed a particular interest in biology. Some of his scientific theories can seem strange to modern minds: the proposal, for example, that thinking occurs in the human heart rather than the brain, and that flies can spontaneously burst into existence out of piles of dung. Others of his views sit very uncomfortably with modern beliefs, such as the notion that natural hierarchies exist (he considered people like himself to be naturally "better formed" than slaves or women), and the claim that "males have more teeth than females in the case of men, sheep, goats, and swine"—which suggests that as well as being sexist, he was bad at counting.

IBN RUSHD (1126–1198)

In the Western tradition, the Andalusian Muslim philosopher Ibn Rushd is often called Averroes, or simply "The Commentator." He worked as a physician and magistrate in Córdoba, and produced a number of highly influential theological and philosophical treatises. Much of his work focused on metaphysical debates about Allah—and one of his central legacies was his defense against the claim, made by Ash'ari theologians like Al-Ghazali, that philosophical analyses were irreligious. In response to Al-Ghazali's *Tahāfut al-Falāsifa* (*The Incoherence of the Philosophers*, c. 1100), Ibn Rushd wrote *Tahāfut al-Tahāfut* (*The Incoherence of Incoherence*, c. 1100), arguing that philosophical thought could harmonize with Islamic faith. It is for his commentaries on Aristotle that Ibn Rushd is perhaps best known in European philosophies, and without his careful unpicking of the original Greek texts, it is unlikely that Thomas Aquinas and other medieval scholastics would have amounted to very much. Ibn Rushd incorporated Aristotelian ideas into Islamic thought, and the scholastics used Aristotle's hylomorphism in much the same way with Catholic doctrine.

ELISABETH OF BOHEMIA (1618–1680)

Elisabeth Simmern van Pallandt was born into turbulent times. When she was two, her father, Frederick V, lost his throne and the family was forced into exile in The Hague, under the protection of Maurice of Nassau. There, Elisabeth excelled in her education—politics, science, logic, and philosophy – but became frustrated at sitting on the sidelines. In 1643, she decided to write to one of the biggest philosophical names of the day, René Descartes (who had served in Maurice's Dutch States Army). So began a mutually productive and stimulating correspondence. Elisabeth questioned Descartes about his views on immaterial substances (how do the emotions or passions effect changes in material objects?)—and in light of their discussions, Descartes wrote *The Passions of the Soul* (1649), also dedicating to her his *Principles of Philosophy* (1644). Their correspondence lasted until Descartes's death in 1650. Elisabeth lived and thrived for another 30 years, working to regain some of the political power lost by her hapless father, and eventually becoming the highly influential Abbess of Herford Convent in Saxony.

SALLY HASLANGER (1955–)

Born in Connecticut, the American metaphysician Sally Haslanger was raised as a Christian Scientist. As such, she was introduced at an early age to idealist suspicions of the material world. Christian Scientists hold that "all is mind, all is God"—and Haslanger has since explained that this way of seeing reality heavily influenced her approach to analytic metaphysics. Where her contemporaries at the University of Virginia and the University of California were in thrall to the dominant materialistic accounts ("all is matter"), Haslanger was less sure, and for this reason she became interested in entities typically sidelined in Western metaphysical inquiry—specifically, social objects. There is a well-established tradition in Euro-American metaphysics that dismisses societies, social groups, and the connections between them as metaphysically uninteresting "constructs." Haslanger's view is that not only are such things really real, but also that discussions about them are considerably more important to us than, for instance, ancient debates about how many angels can dance on the head of a pin.

HYLOMORPHISM

THE MAIN CONCEPT | Look around and you'll find reality is populated by all kinds of stuff. There are sights (colors), sounds (music), and feelings (the sense of dread). There are artifacts (chairs) and arbitrary jumbles of stuff (trash heaps). Then there are living things, like ducks and geese and me and you. Writing in the third century BCE, Aristotle thought these different things exist in different ways. Each has their own "metaphysical character." In *De Anima* (350 BCE), Aristotle suggested that—in contrast to artifacts and qualities—living things are more substantial. They're "primary substances." Primary substances have two metaphysical components, which are inextricably interlinked—"matter" (*hyle*) and "form" (*morphe*). For hylomorphists, matter is the stuff that things are made out of, and form is the way that matter is configured. This is often explained in relation to artifacts; a bronze statue of a cat, for instance, is made out of matter (bronze) and formed in a certain way (in the shape of a cat). But form is more than just shape—it's the manner of being. A statue of a cat may be the shape of a cat, but it's not a cat. The form of a cat includes the way it walks, scratches, and purrs when it has its belly rubbed. It's the cat's whole mode of being.

DRILL DOWN | Aristotle's metaphysical picture has had considerable influence in the history of philosophy. Following the work of Islamic philosopher Ibn Rushd, theologians like Thomas Aquinas and Duns Scotus attempted to incorporate hylomorphism into mainstream Christian doctrine. Hylomorphism came to underpin the dominant intellectual movement of the Middle Ages, known as "scholasticism." As well as informing scientific ideas about organic growth and development, Aquinas and Scotus found the split between form and matter to be helpful in explaining the doctrine of resurrection, where dead bodies are reimbued with life, and transubstantiation, where matter of one sort (the Eucharist) is turned into matter of another sort (the Body of Christ).

THE VIRTUOUS PERSON
Page 26
SCIENTIFIC KNOWLEDGE
Page 102
ESSENTIALISM
Page 140

SWITCH UP | *Metaphysics is supposed to be objective, but as feminist scholars Eve Browning Cole and Charlotte Witt have indicated, Aristotle's work on reality has a pronounced political dimension. Nowhere is this more evident than his hylomorphic schema, which positions societal norms as natural features of the world. So in Aristotle's now-controversial reality, some humans are less well formed than others: in contrast to Greek men, women and slaves are naturally "deformed."*

ETERNITY

THE MAIN CONCEPT | When did the cosmos come into existence? Not the Earth or our Galaxy or the Universe. When did everything begin? Philosophers have been puzzling over this question since the dawn of time— or at least since the days of Parmenides, in the fifth century BCE. Few, however, have examined it with such careful attention as the Persian philosophers Al-Rāzī and Al-Farabi, and the Arabic philosopher Al-Kindī, working in the seventh and eighth centuries CE. Their interests, which found their way into the Western tradition through the expansion of Islamic caliphates, focused on a particular problem: how can an eternal being like Allah—a being who exists outside time—bring something, like the cosmos, into existence? The act of creation involves change, and change can only happen within time. It makes no sense to talk of change when there's no before or after. Al-Farabi, prefiguring the thoughts of Ibn Rushd (Averroes), got around this puzzle by saying that the cosmos is itself eternal—but in a different way to Allah. The cosmos exists within time, yet exists for all time, "bi-directionally," extending infinitely into the past and the future. Thus, Al-Farabi thought, the problem is resolved. The cosmos has always existed, so Allah need never have brought it into existence.

DRILL DOWN | Some maintain that Allah brought time into existence. But to say that time has a starting point suggests there was a previous point (or time) when it didn't exist. This was a conundrum that puzzled Al-Rāzī—and his solution to it has had considerable influence in European thought. In *On Metaphysics*, Al-Rāzī drew a distinction between absolute and relative time to solve the puzzle. Time begins at the first moment of relative time—time relative to the cosmos. If it were possible to step outside the cosmos, or what we call "space and time," we would understand that the cosmos itself exists in a spatial and temporal void, or "absolute" space and absolute time. This difference (supposedly) allows us to mark "the start of" time.

SWITCH UP | *It's not hard to see how this discussion, had over a millennium ago in the Islamic world, has impacted modern-day science. Newtonian mechanics depends heavily on a similar distinction between absolute and relative time—and this same distinction is the framework on which hangs Einstein's musings about temporal relativity. Eternity is a topic of perennial interest.*

SUBSTANCE DUALISM

THE MAIN CONCEPT | Substance dualism is the view that the world is made up of two distinct types of substance: thinking things (in the Latin, *res cogitans*) and extended, material things (*res extensa*). Dualism has a long history, stretching back to (and beyond) Platonic philosophy, but the most famous popularizer of the view is probably Descartes. In his 1641 treatise *The Meditations on First Philosophy*, Descartes opposed the prevailing dogma of the scholastics, who held that all things are mixed-up hylomorphic composites (form and matter being inseparable). Descartes claimed that thinking substances are metaphysically independent of material things—an idea that works well with the Christian concept of the soul. He also denied that all bodies are connected to thinking things. Most entities, from everyday artifacts to nonhuman animals, are just matter. As such, the physical behaviors of bicycles and birds can be explained exclusively by reference to the mechanics of material interactions. It's only in the case of humans (and angels and God) that *res cogitans* comes into play. Descartes's *Cogito*— "I think, therefore I am"—is often seen as part of an epistemological argument; however, by proving the existence of a thinking thing, but not a bodily thing, Descartes was also making a metaphysical point: *res cogitans* is separate from *res extensa*.

DRILL DOWN | Princess Elisabeth of Bohemia wasn't so sure about substance dualism. A long-time collaborator of Descartes, she repeatedly raised questions about the supposed distinction between mind and body. In particular, she focused on the means by which these apparently distinct substances might causally interact. Mechanical laws of the material world suggest that matter can only be moved by other matter. Thinking things, however, are immaterial things. So how can they causally interact with material things? How can the movements of the mind result in movements of the body? Or, vice versa, how can the conditions of the body lead (as they sometimes do) to impact on our cognitive processes?

SKEPTICISM
Page 88

HYLOMORPHISM
Page 120

PERSONAL IDENTITY
Page 128

SWITCH UP | *The seventeenth-century German philosopher Gottfried Wilhelm Leibniz bypassed the problem of mind–body causation by invoking what he called "pre-established harmony." The mental world appears to interact with the physical world because God has programmed these different elements to harmonize with each other. Just as a preprogrammed synth melody harmonizes with other instruments in a song, mind and body harmonize without interacting.*

PHENOMENOLOGY

THE MAIN CONCEPT | Developed as an antidote
to the scientistic metaphysical musings of the late
nineteenth century, phenomenology is the study of human
experience—of phenomena; of the way the world and
its constituents appear to us. Among its earliest advocates
were the Austrian philosopher Edmund Husserl and his
student Edith Stein. Their interests lay in examining
the structures of our first-person experience of reality.
How do inanimate objects, like chairs, figure differently
in our consciousness to living beings like other humans?
How do our experiences of other humans figure differently
to those of ourselves? Phenomenologists say that there
are temporal, spatial, and emotional aspects to such
phenomena—and that our experiences of these depend
on us being the kinds of creatures (embodied, three-
dimensional organisms) that we are. Mapping out
aspects of consciousness is a tricky project, since it's
something in which we are utterly immersed; nevertheless,
phenomenologists have identified organizing features,
such as the intentional aspect of consciousness (how
consciousness is always about things), and its temporal
aspects (how experiences unfold for us). Phenomenologists
are interested in the reality of our experiences themselves,
not whether they accurately map the world beyond them.
They can study the pain felt in a finger, just as much as
the pain experienced by the amputee in a phantom limb.

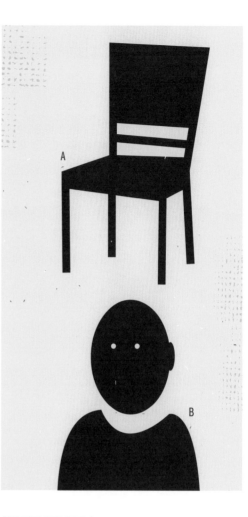

DRILL DOWN | One prominent twentieth-century phenomenologist was the Martinican thinker Frantz Fanon. In *Black Skin, White Masks* (1952), Fanon analyzed the lived experience of being seen as black in a white supremacist society—the "negrification," as he called it, of individuals by others. For Fanon, the phenomenon had particular characteristics and constituted a specific form of violence. Most of all, it encouraged what he called "alienation," the detachment of oneself from one's self. People experience themselves as self-directed, reasoning beings, but in a white supremacist society, people racialized as black are told they are otherwise. This suffocating and pervasive racism distances them from their experiences of themselves in what Fanon described as a form of "psychological colonization."

SWITCH UP | *The French existentialist Simone de Beauvoir treated gender rather than race as the founding category of phenomenological inquiry. She was interested in our lived experience as women or as men. In* The Second Sex *(1949), she brought the gendered body to the fore as an object of phenomenological investigation. What is it to experience the world "as a woman"?*

PERSONAL IDENTITY

THE MAIN CONCEPT | The personal identity debate, which finds early form in John Locke's *Essay Concerning Human Understanding* (1689) is, unsurprisingly, about identity. Identity means different things: it can mean "character" (as in "fake identity") or it can refer to the logical relation symbolized by the "=" (equals) symbol. This debate, then, is about the identity of identities. What is it that makes you identical with the toddler you once were and the old person you may become? How do we track a person—a thinking, characterful, self-reflecting being—through time and space? Locke's answer, which remains popular in the English-speaking tradition, is that personal identity is determined by continued consciousness. You're the same person as the child in those birthday photos because the thinking being that experienced that first birthday "persisted" to experience second, third, and fourth birthdays. The conscious entity continued, and this continuity is evidenced by experiential memory. The fact that you remember, from a first-person perspective, what you were doing 30 minutes ago, indicates that you had those experiences. For Locke, this guarantees personal identity in a way that bodily continuity doesn't—if all your memories and beliefs were taken out of one body and transported to another, you the person would go with them.

DRILL DOWN | To flesh out his account of personal identity, Locke told tales of "soul migration." More recently, philosophers have told stories of "brain transplantations"; the brain is the repository of memories, they say, so wherever your brain goes, you go too. The British philosopher Susan James, however, is unimpressed with these musings. For her, they sideline the embodied nature of our experience. What about those memories that are intimately connected to the bodies they were formed in: for example, the experience of breaking your leg, or the surgery you had to fix it? Lockean fantasies simplify complex embodied phenomena, creating an alien and disconcerting picture of a discrete, potentially disembodied "consciousness."

SWITCH UP | *In the late twentieth century, Euro-American philosophers like Derek Parfit began to pay greater attention to non-Western discussions of personhood. Recent Western work has been enriched through attention to Buddhist examinations of the self (like that found in the third-century CE text the* Milinda Pañha). *The Buddhist notion of* anattā, *or "no-self," stands as an interesting comparison to Western "reductionist" conceptions of the person as nothing more than a brain, body, and associated mental and physical events.*

THE SOCIAL CONTRACT
Page 18
STANDPOINT THEORY
Page 104
BIOLOGICAL CREATION
Page 132

LOGIC

THE MAIN CONCEPT | Logic can be understood in a variety of different ways. When analytic philosophers talk about logic they are, broadly speaking, referring to a specific system of reasoning built around certain laws and principles. You must be consistent; the conclusion of your argument must follow from your premises. These are the laws of logic that you are supposed to abide by if your argument—philosophical or otherwise—is to preserve truth. One of the central tenets in the Western system is the "principle of non-contradiction" (or PNC). This holds that two propositions cannot both be true in the same sense at the same time. So, if I say "I am writing and I am not writing," the two propositions are, in relation to truth, mutually exclusive. They contradict one another, so one of them has to be false. The PNC has been orthodoxy in European philosophy for thousands of years, but it has generated puzzles for just as long. One such puzzle is the "liar's paradox," captured in the following sentence: "The sentence is false." If the sentence is true, then it is false. But if it is false, it is true. It is self-contradictory, and thus paradoxical.

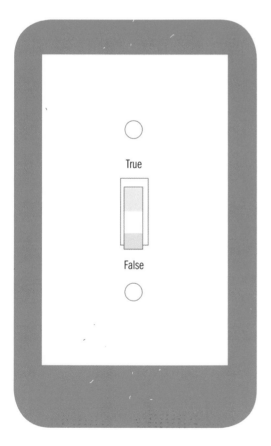

DRILL DOWN | The PNC is mainstream in European philosophy. But not everyone thinks contradiction is anathema to solid reasoning. Rather than rejecting "dialetheia"—sentences that are both true and false—other, non-Western philosophies have accepted and productively analyzed self-contradictory statements. The Indian philosopher B. K. Matilal showed how ancient Indian logic permitted four possibilities in relation to the "truth value" of statements: true, false, neither true nor false, or both true and false. Buddhist and Jain philosophies are similarly flexible. Following Matilal, Western philosophers such as Graham Priest have begun to develop "paraconsistent" logics—systems that accommodate contradictions instead of excluding them wholesale.

SWITCH UP | *Where does logic come from? According to a prominent, Eurocentric story, it has its origins in ancient Greece—specifically in the work of Aristotle. Jonardon Ganeri is one of a number of scholars challenging this picture by drawing attention to the appearance of logistic reasoning in ancient Hindu philosophy. Did Greek and Hindu logic develop independently? Or, as Mary Everest Boole has suggested, did these intellectual traditions cross-pollinate?*

BIOLOGICAL CREATION

THE MAIN CONCEPT | Philosophers have long been interested in how organisms come into existence. These days, such things are often debated within the sphere of the philosophy of biology rather than metaphysics, but the roots of these two subdisciplines are closely interlinked. As we know from *De Anima* (see page 120), Aristotle saw metaphysical and biological inquiry to be two sides of the same coin. He proposed a hylomorphic "flowerpot theory of pregnancy" (as it was labeled by US philosopher Caroline Whitbeck), in which women were the passive material vessels for an activating male form, or "seed." Aristotle's view is now understood to be both deeply sexist and metaphysically suspect—but echoes still sound. Philosophers such as Elselijn Kingma and Suki Finn reject the flowerpot view in favor of "mereological" analyses of biological creation. Mereology is the study of parts (*meros* in Greek) and wholes. Kingma's view is that when a woman becomes pregnant, she gains an extra part, instead of becoming host, or container, to another human whole. A fetus, she believes, is a part—in the same way that organs are parts—but a special one, which eventually detaches and becomes whole.

DRILL DOWN | Metaphysics is often thought to be undertaken in ivory towers—but it's clear that our views on biological creation have pressing, real-world relevance. Whether we think fetuses are parts of women's bodies or not will affect our views about abortion; the rights of a woman over her own body (and her own body parts) are applied differently to the rights of parents over their children. Our views about the precise moment of creation also have bearing here. If you believe, as Elselijn Kingma does, that a fetus is a special detaching part, you'll need to have a view about when such parts become wholes. Is it at birth? In which case, where would premature births figure in this account?

SWITCH UP | *L. A. Paul and Chitra Ramaswamy have both brought attention to the distinctive, mind-expanding experience of pregnancy. As Paul puts it, pregnancy has a "transformative phenomenological character"—which means that it allows the mother to grasp reality in a different way. Many women will attest to this— but nonbiological parents may object to the claim that biological mothers have epistemic insights that others lack.*

SOCIAL ONTOLOGY

THE MAIN CONCEPT | Social ontology is the investigation of social entities and relations, ontology being the study of being. In the past, metaphysicians may have dismissed things such as football clubs and legal systems as unworthy of metaphysical analysis. Why? Because they're social constructs—they're dependent on human interests, or emerge from human practices. The social ontologist, however, says that something being a social construct doesn't make it any less real. They're still part of reality and have undeniable real-world effects. Take social groups. You may say, of course, that there's "no such thing as society" and that social groups are nothing over and above the individuals that make them up. But it's hard to deny that they have causal powers that individuals lack. A group can be democratic, or it can go to war. And groups can survive a constant exchange of their parts—a soccer team consists of a certain set of members but they're constantly fluctuating, and at a certain point, none of the original members will remain in the team. Social ontologists are interested in the metaphysical character of these social entities. Can such groups have beliefs and intentions? Are they accountable or responsible in the same way that individuals are? And are there metaphysical laws that determine how these social categories and objects are constructed?

DRILL DOWN | It is not uncommon to hear people making ontological claims about group membership. Often, these claims are false. Take, for instance, the claim that there are essential differences between genders. This is what it is to be a woman; that is what it is to be a man. The guiding thought is that there are real, naturally occurring biological properties that members of one group have, and members of another group lack. Social ontologists point out that the science behind these claims has been disproved—but they go even further. They analyze the modes of social construction and investigate how the social entity "woman" came into existence in the first place, whether through collective action, institutional practice, or as a function of language.

MORAL REALISM
Page 42
THE CATEGORY OF "ART"
Page 52
IGNORANCE
Page 90

SWITCH UP | *In her book* Resisting Reality *(2012), Sally Haslanger encourages us to engage with oppressive social constructs—by seeing them as real. She writes: "We should not resist seeing the reality that we should, in fact, resist; in fact, disclosing that reality is a crucial precondition for successful resistance." Combating troublesome social constructs requires recognizing they exist to begin with.*

NATURAL KINDS

THE MAIN CONCEPT | Often, when we're categorizing the contents of reality—for instance, people who like chocolate versus people who don't—we do so according to human interest. Sometimes, however, the world seems to divide things up for us. There appear to be natural kinds—kinds that exist in the natural realm, independent of human concerns. Animal species are, ostensibly, a good example of this. Chickens are a particular kind of bird, *Gallus gallus domesticus*; irrespective of human observation, they will always be a different kind of natural thing from dogs (*Canis familiaris*). Birds of a feather flock together, irrespective of what we think about them. The same goes for other species—*Homo sapiens* included. The "natural kind realist" thinks that there are, as Plato put it, "joints" in the natural world, and the task of the philosopher and scientist is to cut nature at these joints rather than drawing arbitrary distinctions across categories. This view is closely connected to a certain type of essentialism (see page 140), which holds that a category is based on a particular essence—for example, the essence shared by all cats that belong to the species *Felis catus*. It is this essence, some think, that biologists are investigating when they conduct research into the genetic makeup of different organisms.

DRILL DOWN | Philosophers of science, such as Nancy Cartwright and John Dupré, have shown that the biological realm is much more complicated than Plato assumed. In *The Disorder of Things* (1993), Dupré argues that species boundaries are far from hard and fast. For one thing, the Darwinian theory of evolution indicates that species are not static but evolve over time, so any supposed natural categories are in flux. For another thing, genetic makeup and morphological character (the appearance of organisms) vary massively within species. So it's difficult, if not impossible, to isolate "essential" genetic markers. Consequently, Dupré advocates "promiscuous realism," the view that reality may be partitioned in a number of different, yet equally real, ways.

SWITCH UP | *From Aristotle onward, philosophers have tried to demarcate species boundaries alongside racial boundaries. Immanuel Kant's 1775 treatise "On the Different Races of Man" is an egregious, but not isolated, example of this. On the grounds that there are no race-distinguishing genes and huge genetic variation within apparent racial groups, specialists in this field Naomi Zack and Michael O. Hardimon have argued that we should abandon any biological notion of race.*

CULTURAL RELATIVISM
Page 74

THE MEDICAL GAZE
Page 106

ESSENTIALISM
Page 140

THE SORITES PARADOX

THE MAIN CONCEPT | The sorites paradox was first posed by Eubulides of Miletus in the fourth century BCE. "Sorites" comes from the Greek word for "heap"—as in a heap of salt or sand. It seems obvious, said Eubulides, that if you remove a grain of sand from a heap of 100,000 grains you'll still be left with a heap. So, the following appears relatively uncontroversial: the removal of a single grain cannot cause a heap to go out of existence. However, imagine you keep taking away single grains until you've got a much, much smaller heap. When does it go out of existence? When you've got ten grains? Or nine? Or two? The paradox emerges from the tension between two apparently uncontroversial claims. First, that the removal of a single grain cannot cause a heap to disappear. Second, that the heap clearly disappears. This is a problem with vagueness: heaps have vague boundaries—so it's hard to say when a heap ceases to be a heap. Nor is this a problem reserved exclusively for heaps; there are also other vague spatial boundaries (when, for example, do shorts become pants?), and vague temporal boundaries (when does a human come into existence?). The paradox prompts a peculiar form of metaphysical blurry vision; the more you look at reality, the fuzzier things become.

DRILL DOWN | The sorites paradox has prompted the development of a special kind of logic, which the Persian mathematician and computer scientist Lotfi Aliasker Zadeh called "fuzzy logic." While mainstream, Western "bivalent" logic holds that all statements have only two "valences" (values)—true or false—fuzzy logic states that there is a graded spectrum, stretching from absolute truth to absolute falsity. Between these two extremes, things can be half true, and half false. In the case of the sorites paradox, claims about the heap can become false, by small increments. As you're taking grains away, little by little, you're making the statement "This is a heap" less and less true.

SWITCH UP | *The American philosopher Delia Graff Fara articulated what is becoming an increasingly popular view of vagueness. When we experience things as vague, she said, it's because our attitudes toward these entities are constantly shifting. Our views about when a heap ceases to be a heap depend on our motivations for labeling it as such. Vagueness is interest-relative.*

ESSENTIALISM

THE MAIN CONCEPT | Essentialism is, roughly, the view that things have essences. All the entities around us have intrinsic properties or structures that are essential to them, which make them what they are. An intrinsic property is a property possessed by an object independently of other issues—in contrast to extrinsic properties, which objects have in relation to other objects (like "being underneath"). The essentialist holds that there are properties that, for instance, dogs have that are inessential and extrinsic. A dog's name being Molly is changeable. Then there are intrinsic properties that are essential, which constitute the dogginess of the dog, and which we can't change if we want the entity to continue existing. If you're a species essentialist, you'll likely say that there are genetic structures or morphological features that—if Molly lacked—would cause her to cease being a dog. The American philosopher Saul Kripke spoke in more general terms, stating in *Naming and Necessity* (1980) that a property is essential to an object if "it is true of that object in any case where it would have existed." This includes properties like species membership (Molly wouldn't have been Molly if she hadn't been a dog) but also things like having the parents one has or being born in a particular time and place.

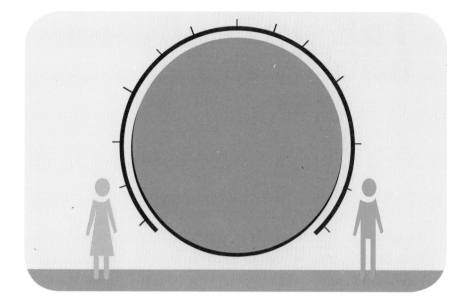

DRILL DOWN | What things are essential to you? In *Gender Trouble* (1990), Judith Butler urged us to think deeply about our seemingly essential attributes. Are you a man? Are you a woman? If you think you're a man, do you think you're essentially manly? Butler suggests that, though traditionally construed as essential, these features—masculinity and femininity—are in some ways accidental. Gender—as opposed to biological sex—is conferred on us by culture. It's a role, a performance. As Simone de Beauvoir puts it, "One is not born, but rather becomes, a woman"—so one may, perhaps, cease to be a man or a woman, and continue to exist.

SWITCH UP | *Are you male or female? Biologically, you may say, you are clearly male or female ("check the genitals!"). The American gender and queer theorist Judith Jack Halberstam disagrees and points to a wealth of scientific studies that show that rather than a strict binary (male/female) there is huge variation in human biological sexes. So maybe even your sex is more complicated than you thought?*

QUEER THEORY
Page 40

PERSONAL IDENTITY
Page 128

SOCIAL ONTOLOGY
Page 134

THE ONTOLOGICAL ARGUMENT

THE MAIN CONCEPT | The Greek word *ontos* means "being," so an ontological argument is an argument or a proof about being or existence. In the Western context, such arguments are typically aimed at proving the existence of one entity in particular: God. Probably the most well-known ontological argument was put forward by the French theologian Anselm of Canterbury. Written around the time of the Norman Conquest in the eleventh century, Anselm's *Proslogion* (c. 1077) offers a proof of God's existence that relies on an analysis of the definition of a supremely perfect being. God, Anselm said, can be defined as "that than which nothing greater can be conceived." By definition, then, God is perfect. But what if God only exists in our minds? Anselm suggested that existence in reality is greater than existence in the imagination. (What's more perfect than the dream of a delicious chocolate? A delicious chocolate that exists, which you can actually eat!) Yet, he went on, if that were true, and God doesn't exist, then we can surely conceive of a being greater than God. Specifically: one that exists. But God is a being "that than which nothing greater can be conceived." Unless we want to abandon that uncontroversial defining premise, we must say that God, as a perfect being, exists in reality and not just our minds.

DRILL DOWN | According to Anselm, existence is a form of perfection. But his contemporary, the Benedictine monk Gaunilo of Marmoutiers, disagreed. In his treatise *On Behalf of the Fool* (c. 1078), Gaunilo presented a refutation of Anselm's proof in the form of the "lost island" argument. Gaunilo asks us to imagine a perfect island, "that than which no greater island can be conceived." Since existing things are greater than nonexisting things, this island's failure to exist would make it possible to conceive of something greater—in other words, an island that exists in reality. By Anselm's reasoning, this should prove the island's existence— but Gaunilo says the perfect island demonstrably doesn't exist. So Anselm's argument is unsound.

THE PARADOX OF FICTION
Page 66
EMPIRICISM
Page 94
***A PRIORI* KNOWLEDGE**
Page 96

SWITCH UP | *In his* Guide for the Perplexed *(c. 1190), the twelfth-century Jewish philosopher Moses Maimonides presented an alternative "cosmological" argument for God's existence. All corporeal things are finite, he said, and finite things can only contain finite power. As such, they're destined to run out of energy and stop moving. But the planets keep turning, infinitely, so they must've been caused by something with infinite power. That something, he said, is God.*

ORGANISMS & ARTIFACTS

THE MAIN CONCEPT | Organisms are generally thought to be the end product of naturally occurring processes of reproduction. Artifacts, by contrast—spoons, cars, and umbrellas—are the things that organisms make. The American philosopher Lynne Rudder Baker said that artifacts can only really be made by self-conscious, intending agents (notably humans). So the Hoover Dam may be an artifact, while a beaver's dam may not. Yet, even with these clarifications, advances in technology have started to blur these categorial lines. Scientists standardly grow new strains of bacteria in tanks. Are these living products artifacts? Or organisms? What about biomedical procedures; how much interference can "natural beings" suffer before they start to "denature"? On the whole, artifacts have replaceable parts (if your computer's battery runs out, you can get a new one). Indeed, the connections between parts and wholes are so loose you can swap an artifact's bits around almost at will (a cell phone and its cover, for example). Organisms, by contrast, have always appeared to be more strongly unified. We can't just go around replacing organs left, right, and center . . . except that we can. Drawn along by the lure of science fiction, medical technologies have developed bionic limbs, electronic implants, and organ transplantation. Are we becoming artifactual beings?

DRILL DOWN | The term "cyborg" is short for "cybernetic organism"—a being, like Robocop, with both organic and cybernetic parts. In her 1984 essay "A Cyborg Manifesto," Donna Haraway examined the challenge cyborgs pose to the established categories of organism and artifact: the old, oppositional dualisms—mind/body, self/other, and organism/artifact—are dissolved in the fluid body of the cyborg. N. Katherine Hayles, in writing about the Internet, has pointed out how the cyborg's influence grows stronger when we think about our "online lives." Connecting on the Web, our lives are becoming less discretely located.

SWITCH UP | *Biomedical advances raise important metaphysical and ethical issues. Anyone who's watched the movie* Gattaca *will wonder about the ontological status of "designer" babies (whose genetic makeup has been selected by the parents-to-be). Like cyborgs, they appear to blur the organic and artifactual lines. What societal impact will the availability of such costly processes be? Will "human enhancement" become the preserve of the rich?*

TAKING THINGS FURTHER

The focus of this book is very much on the Euro-American tradition. However, as mentioned in the general introduction, this did not develop in isolation. The Euro-American tradition exists alongside, and overlaps, many others from around the world. It is therefore worth concluding with a brief consideration of some of these other schools of thought, in order to get a better sense of the global philosophical landscape. We have also included the titles of works that will provide good starting points for further reading in each case.

Latin America

There were a variety of rich traditions of philosophical inquiry in what some refer to as pre-Columbian Latin America (South American countries before the arrival of Christopher Columbus and the Spanish Empire). The Andean and Aztec traditions, for instance, devoted much attention to the nature of reality, existence, ethical conduct, and the concept of *camac* (life force). The Andean traditions can be split into Inca and non-Inca schools, the latter of which manifests differently in different *ayllus* (social groups). Inca Andean philosophy refers to the view of the *amautas* (a Quecha word meaning "sages" or "poet-philosophers"). To find out more, check out *A Companion to Latin American Philosophy*, edited by Susana Nuccetelli, Ofelia Schutte, and Otávio Bueno.

Africa

Philosophical thought flourished in Kemet (Ancient Egypt, in the centuries between 3000 BCE and 300 BCE) and in Kush (between 1000 BCE and 600 BCE). Thinkers such as Imhotep, Hordjedef, and Lady Peseshet developed philosophical systems that examined metaphysical, physical, and epistemological issues. In Nigeria, the Yoruba traditions emerged to discuss ethical values, morality, and the nature of knowledge—and "sage philosophy" (as described by twentieth-century philosopher Henry Odera Oruka) still stands as a distinctive methodological approach to the construction of philosophical systems. We recommend reading *A Companion to African Philosophy*, edited by Kwasi Wiredu, and Lewis Gordon's *Introduction to Africana Philosophy*.

China

Chinese philosophy has a long and varied history reaching back to the *I Ching*, a divination manual written in the twelfth century BCE, and the subject of innumerable philosophical and cosmological commentaries. Confucianism is another major strand of Chinese philosophy (originating with Confucius in 500 BCE), as is Taoism (which takes Laozi's *Tao Te Ching* as one of its key texts). Other philosophical schools include Chinese Naturalism, Mohism, and Legalism. For a guide to these traditions, have a look at *A Source Book in Chinese Philosophy,* with entries compiled by Wing-Tsit Chan.

The Arab world

The Arabic schools of thought emerged from the Arab world, spanning Iberia, North Africa, and Persia. In 700 CE, Arabic philosophy was dominated by theological debate relating to Islam, but also Christianity and Judaism. The ninth to twelfth century CE constituted the classical period of Arabic philosophy, with thinkers like Ibn Sina (also known as Avicenna), Al-Kindī, and Al-Farabi discussing metaphysical, logical, ethical, mathematical, and even pharmacological issues. Ibn Rushd is well known for dealing with the relation between *falsafa* (philosophy) and religion. *The Cambridge Companion to Arabic Philosophy*, edited by Peter Adamson and Richard Taylor, offers a good introduction to some of the Arabic schools.

India

Well before Plato and Aristotle, Ancient India boasted a thriving philosophical culture. The Vedantic, Yogic, and Śramanic Hindu schools developed during the Vedic Period (1500–500 BCE), and examined metaphysical, theological, and epistemological concerns, often stemming from discussions found in the central Hindu texts known as the Upanishads. The Indian philosophical traditions also take logic and logical systems as their focus (see, for example, the texts produced by the Vaisheshika school in the second century BCE) as well as various forms of atomism, dualism, and monistic idealism. Have a look at *The Oxford Handbook of Indian Philosophy*, edited by Jonardon Ganeri, to find out more.

GLOSSARY

A POSTERIORI—describes statements encapsulating information supplied by the senses, rather than deriving from reason alone (posterior to experience).

A PRIORI—describes statements whose justification relies on reason alone, rather than knowledge gleaned from the senses (prior to experience).

AGENT—an individual capable of choosing how to act.

ANALYTIC/CONTINENTAL—the (controversial) distinction between different kinds of philosophy—those putatively practiced in the US/UK and those on the Continent (of Europe).

ARGUMENT—an interpersonal exchange ("you and I had an argument") or a set of sentences, one of which (the conclusion) putatively follows from the others (premises).

AUTONOMOUS—a being is autonomous when it is self-directing or self-legislating (i.e., when it sets its own laws—or, in the Greek, *nomos*).

CATEGORICAL IMPERATIVE—deriving from Kant's ethical theory, this term refers to an unconditional moral obligation.

CONCEPT—an abstract idea. It is sometimes distinguished from "conception," which is a particular manifestation of an abstract idea (e.g., you can have a particular conception of the concept of justice).

COUNTER-ARGUMENT—an argument specifically geared toward challenging the premises and/or conclusion of another argument.

COUNTER-EXAMPLE—an example used to undermine an argument, claim, or thesis (e.g., a bat is a counter-example to the claim that only birds can fly).

DEDUCTION—a form of reasoning in which a particular conclusion is understood to follow necessarily from one or more specific premises.

DEHUMANIZATION—a process by which people are framed as less than human (i.e., as animals or objects), and, as such, deserving of inhumane treatment.

DUALISM—a term used to refer to a system or conceptual framework composed of two typically exclusive and contrasting elements (e.g., mind–body dualism).

EPISTEMIC—describes some relation to knowledge (e.g., epistemic oppression is oppression caused by a system of knowledge).

EPISTEMOLOGICAL—related to the area of philosophy known as epistemology (study of knowledge).

FALLACY—a mistaken belief or invalid form of argument.

IDEALISM—in metaphysics, the thesis that nothing exists apart from minds and their ideas. In politics, the thesis that ideas are primary determinants of social realities.

IMPLICATION—a conclusion that seems to follow from certain premises, but isn't explicitly stated.

INDUCTION—a form of reasoning where a conclusion is thought to be strongly supported (but not logically guaranteed) by a sufficient number of observations.

INFERENCE—the process of moving, via reasoned argument, from accepted premises to a conclusion.

INFERENCE TO THE BEST EXPLANATION—a form of reasoning where a given explanation is thought to best explain a particular phenomenon by virtue of meeting certain criteria, e.g., being the simplest, most plausible explanation.

"INFERS THAT" VS. "IMPLIES THAT"—a thinker infers a conclusion from a set of evidence or premises; a set of evidence or premises implies a conclusion. Many people confuse the two.

JUDGMENT—the mental act by which one person holds an action or entity against, e.g., certain moral standards.

KNOWER—an individual who possesses knowledge of a given domain (e.g., a teacher).

MATERIALISM—in metaphysics, the thesis that nothing exists apart from matter. In politics, the thesis that material conditions are primary determinants of social realities.

MAXIM—a pithy statement that expresses a purported truth or rule.

METAPHYSICS—the area of academic philosophy that deals with the nature of reality (including, but not limited to, how it is structured and what entities exist).

NECESSARY/SUFFICIENT CONDITIONS—something is a necessary condition for a particular situation if that situation can only exist if that special something is present. A sufficient condition is one where its fulfillment is by itself enough to bring about the situation.

NECESSITY/CONTINGENCY—in discussions around what is possible and what is not, necessity refers to those things that must always be the case (in every possible world), while contingency refers to those things that are possible but not of necessity.

NORM—a term that loosely refers to something that is standard or normal. More precisely, it can refer to a phenomenon that actively identifies itself as normal (and by extension, classifies other things as abnormal).

OBJECTION—a point of disagreement, usually supported by reasoning, raised in opposition to, e.g., an argument.

ONTOLOGY—from the Greek root, *ontos*, which roughly means "being," ontology refers to a subset of metaphysical discussions typically focused on which entities do and don't exist.

PARADOX—this term loosely describes a statement or state of affairs that, despite appearing absurd or contradictory, is nonetheless true. More technically, a paradox is a set of statements all of which are ostensibly true, but two or more of which contradict each other.

POLITICIZATION—the process by which a subject is either rendered political or considered through a political lens (e.g., philosophers may politicize the manufacture of chocolate by focusing on the slave labor that sustains it).

PRINCIPLE—a rule that is taken to be true and that serves as a guide for, e.g., scientific inquiries or philosophical discussions.

PROPOSITION—this term picks out "that" statements—e.g., "I believe that the world is round," "I hope that I find my shoes."

RATIONAL—that which is thought to be in accordance with reason (as opposed to, e.g., sentiment).

REALISM—a term that applies across topics and picks out those theses where something is taken to be real. In discussions around sense perception, direct realism is the thesis that we have direct access to the real world.

REFUTATION—(putatively) a knock-down response to an argument.

SCHOLASTICISM—the name for a particular philosophical tradition, emerging from the monastic schools in France in the ninth century.

SCIENTISTIC—as opposed to scientific, scientistic refers to an excessive—almost obsessive—focus on science as an arbiter of, e.g., philosophical disputes.

SOUND/UNSOUND—an argument is sound if it is valid and if its premises are actually true.

TABULA RASA—used by the British empiricists, the concept of *tabula rasa* (Latin for "blank slate") encapsulates the idea that we are born without any ideas (innate or otherwise) and learn things (have information inscribed on the tablet) as we grow up.

THESIS—broadly, a claim or theory offered for discussion. More specifically, an essay or dissertation.

THOUGHT EXPERIMENT—rather than going out into the world to test their ideas, philosophers often examine concepts and intuitions by seeing how they might work in imagined scenarios, or "thought experiments."

TRUTH CLAIM—a claim that someone holds to be true.

VALID/INVALID—an argument is valid if it is impossible for its premises to be true and its conclusion false. It is invalid if its premises can be true and the conclusion false.

FURTHER READING

Adamson, Peter, and Richard Taylor (eds.). *The Cambridge Companion to Arabic Philosophy*. Cambridge, UK: Cambridge University Press, 2005.

Anderson, Pamela Sue. *A Feminist Philosophy of Religion*. Oxford, UK: Wiley-Blackwell, 1997.

Appiah, Kwame Anthony. *Cosmopolitanism: Ethics in a World of Strangers*. London: Norton, 2006.

Aristotle. *De Anima*, 350 BCE.

Aristotle. *Nichomachean Ethics*, 340 BCE.

Barker, Meg-John and Julia Scheele. *Queer: A Graphic History*. London: Icon Books, 2016.

Barthes, Roland. "The Death of the Author." In *Aspen*, no. 5–6, 1967.

de Beauvoir, Simone. *The Second Sex*. London: Vintage Publishing, 1949.

Berkeley, George. *Three Dialogues between Hylas and Philonous*, 1713.

Burke, Edmund. *A Vindication of Natural Society and Reflections on the Revolution in France*, 1756.

Chan, Wing-Tsit (trsl.). *A Source Book in Chinese Philosophy*. Princeton, New Jersey: Princeton University Press, 1963.

Code, Lorraine. *Ecological Thinking*. Oxford, UK: Oxford University Press, 2006.

Collins, Patricia Hill. *Black Feminist Thought*. Boston: Hyman, 1990.

Collins, Patricia Hill, and Sirma Bilge. *Intersectionality*. Cambridge, UK: Polity Press, 2016.

Cooper, Anna Julia. *A Voice From the South By a Black Woman of the South*, 1892.

Davis, Angela. *Abolition Democracy: Beyond Empire, Prisons, and Torture*. New York: Seven Stories Press, 2004.

Davis, Lennard J. (ed.). *The Disability Studies Reader*. New York: Routledge, 1997.

Descartes, René. *Meditations & Discourse on Method*, 1641.

Dissanayake, Ellen. *What Is Art For?* Seattle: University of Washington Press, 1988.

Dotson, Kristie. "Conceptualizing Epistemic Oppression." In *Social Epistemology*, vol. 28, 2014.

Du Bois, W. E. B. *The Souls of Black Folk*. Chicago: A. C. McClurg & Co., 1903.

Dupré, John. *The Disorder of Things*. Cambridge, Massachusetts: Harvard University Press, 1993.

Fanon, Frantz. *Black Skin, White Masks*. Paris: Éditions de Seuil, 1952.

Fara, Delia Graff. "Shifting Sands: An Interest Relative Theory of Vagueness." In *Philosophical Topics*, vol. 28, 2000.

Foot, Philippa. "The Problem of Abortion and the Doctrine of Double Effect." In *Oxford Review*, vol. 5, 1967.

Foucault, Michel. *The Birth of the Clinic*. New York: Vintage Books, 1963.

Fricker, Miranda. *Epistemic Injustice: Power and the Ethics of Knowing*. Oxford, UK: Oxford University Press, 2007.

Ganeri, Jonardon. *The Oxford Handbook of Indian Philosophy*. Oxford, UK: Oxford University Press, 2017.

Gardiner, Stephen, et al. *Climate Ethics: Essential Readings*. Oxford, UK: Oxford University Press, 2010.

Gordon, Lewis R. *An Introduction to Africana Philosophy*. Cambridge, UK: Cambridge University Press, 2012.

Halberstam, Judith Jack. *Female Masculinity*. Durham, North Carolina: Duke University Press, 1998.

Haraway, Donna. "A Cyborg Manifesto." In *Socialist Review Collective*, 1984.

Harding, Sandra. *The Feminist Standpoint Theory Reader: Intellectual and Political Controversies*. New York: Routledge, 2004.

Haslanger, Sally. *Resisting Reality*. Oxford, UK: Oxford University Press, 2012.

Hills, Alison. *Do Animals Have Rights?* London: Icon Books, 2005.

hooks, bell. "Eating the Other: Desire and Resistance." In *Black Looks: Race and Representation*. Boston, Massachusetts: South End Press, 1992.

Hume, David. *An Enquiry Concerning Human Understanding*, 1748.

Hume, David. "Of the Standard of Taste," 1757.

Hutcheson, Francis. "Reflections Upon Laughter," 1725.

James, Susan. "Feminism in Philosophy of Mind." In *The Cambridge Companion to Feminism in Philosophy*. Cambridge, UK: Cambridge University Press, 2000.

Kant, Immanuel. *Critique of Judgment*, 1790.

Kant, Immanuel. *Critique of Pure Reason*, 1781.

Kingma, Elselijn. "Lady Parts: The Metaphysics of Pregnancy." In *Metaphysics*. Cambridge, UK: Cambridge University Press, 2018.

Kripke, Saul. *Naming and Necessity*. Cambridge, Massachusetts: Harvard University Press, 1980.

Kuhn, Thomas. *The Structure of Scientific Revolutions*. Chicago: University of Chicago Press, 1962.

Kulka, Tomáš. "Forgeries and Art Evaluation." In *British Journal of Aesthetics*, vol. 29, 2005.

Leibniz, Gottfried Wilhelm. *The Monadology*, 1714.

Locke, John. *Second Treatise on Government*, 1689.

Lorde, Audre. *Sister Outsider*. Berkeley, California: Ten Speed Press, 1984.

Marx, Karl, and Friedrich Engels. *The Communist Manifesto*, 1848.

Matilal, B. K. *Logic, Language and Reality: An Introduction to Indian Philosophical Studies*. Delhi: Motilal Banarsidass, 1985.

Medina, José. *The Epistemology of Resistance.* Oxford, UK: Oxford University Press, 2013.

Mill, John Stuart, and Harriet Taylor-Mill. *On Liberty*, 1859.

Mills, Charles W. *The Racial Contract*. Ithaca, New York: Cornell University Press, 1997.

Ney, Alyssa. *Metaphysics: An Introduction*. New York: Routledge, 2014.

Nguyen, C. Thi, and José P. Zagal. "Good Violence, Bad Violence: The Ethics of Competition in Multiplayer Games." In *Proceedings of the First Joint International DiGRA FDG Conference*, no. 1, vol. 13., 2016.

Nuccetelli, Susana, Ofelia Schutte, and Otávio Bueno (eds.). *A Companion to Latin American Philosophy*. Oxford, UK: Wiley-Blackwell, 2009.

Nussbaum, Martha C. *Creating Capabilites: The Human Development Approach*. Boston, Masachusetts: Harvard University Press, 2013.

Oliver, Kelly. *Witnessing: Beyond Recognition*. Minneapolis, Minnesota: University of Minnesota Press, 2001.

Plato. *The Republic*, 380 BCE.

Rawls, John. *A Theory of Justice*. Boston, Masachusetts: Harvard University Press, 1971.

Rousseau, Jean-Jacques. *The Social Contract*, 1762.

Russell, Bertrand. *The Problems of Philosophy*. New York: H. Holt, 1912.

Said, Edward. *Orientalism*. New York: Pantheon Books, 1978.

Saito, Yuriko. *Everyday Aesthetics*. Oxford, UK: Oxford University Press, 2010.

Saul, Jennifer. "Pornography, Speech Acts, and Context." In *Proceedings of the Aristotelian Society*, vol.106, 2006.

Simplican, Stacy. *The Capacity Contract*. Minneapolis, Minnesota: University of Minnesota Press, 2015.

Tuana, Nancy. "The Speculum of Ignorance." In *Hypatia*, vol. 21, 2006.

Young, Iris Marion. *Justice and the Politics of Difference*. Princeton, New Jersey: Princeton University Press, 1990.

Wimsatt, William, and Munroe Beardsley. "The Intentional Fallacy." In *The Sewanee Review*, vol. 54, 1946.

Wiredu, Kwasi (ed.). *A Companion to African Philosophy*. Oxford, UK: Wiley-Blackwell, 2003.

INDEX

ABOUT THE AUTHORS

Zara Bain has taught philosophy in schools, universities, and colleges, and is currently researching the politics and epistemology of ignorance with funding from the Arts and Humanities Research Council in the UK. She has been published in *Ethics and Education*, *Global Justice*, and *The Philosophers' Magazine* blog. In her spare time, she enjoys testing the theory that anything can be made to look like Nietzsche by adding a handlebar mustache and a pompadour to it.

Adam Ferner has worked in academic philosophy both in France and the UK, but prefers working outside the academy in alternative learning spaces. He has written two books, *Organisms and Personal Identity* (2016) and *Think Differently* (2018), and has published widely in philosophical and popular journals.

Nadia Mehdi works broadly within the traditions of feminist philosophy and philosophy of race. She teaches at both the university and schools level with the University of Sheffield in the UK. Her current research focuses on oppression and resistance at our cultural peripheries and is funded by the White Rose College of the Arts and Humanities.

ACKNOWLEDGMENTS

In writing this book we wanted to track, and to fairly remunerate, the intellectual labor that produced it. As collaborators, Nadia, Zara, and Adam shared the writing and authoring responsibilities. We had additional support from a series of consultants, who commented on chapters and sections: Kristie Dotson, Jonardon Ganeri, Sally Haslanger, Robin James, Aaron Meskin, Charles W. Mills, Chris Meyns, C. Thi Nguyen, Andrew Puzzo, Laurencia Saenz Benavides, and Jeanine Weekes Schroer. We have had productive conversations with, and support from, the editorial team at Ivy Press: Susan Kelly, Claire Saunders, Tom Kitch, Stephanie Evans, and Angela Koo. We would also like to thank and honor: Selma Mehdi, Innes MacLeod, Esther McManus, Daniel Bain, and Rosie Taylor.